Collins

Cambridge IGCSE™

Geography

WORKBOOK

Rebecca Kitchen, Series edited by Alan Parkinson

William Collins' dream of knowledge for all began with the publication of his first book in 1819.
A self-educated mill worker, he not only enriched millions of lives, but also founded a flourishing publishing house.
Today, staying true to this spirit, Collins books are packed with inspiration, innovation and practical expertise.
They place you at the centre of a world of possibility and give you exactly what you need to explore it.

Published by Collins

An imprint of HarperCollins*Publishers*

The News Building, 1 London Bridge Street, London,
SE1 9GF, UK

Macken House, 39/40 Mayor Street Upper, Dublin 1,
D01 C9W8, Ireland

Browse the complete Collins catalogue at
collins.co.uk

© HarperCollins*Publishers* Limited 2025

10 9 8 7 6 5 4 3 2 1

A catalogue record for this publication is available from the British Library.

ISBN 978-0-00-872580-8

All rights reserved. No part of this publication may be reproduced, stored in a retrieval system, or transmitted in any form by any means, electronic, mechanical, photocopying, recording or otherwise, without the prior written permission of the Publisher or a licence permitting restricted copying in the United Kingdom issued by the Copyright Licensing Agency Ltd,
5th Floor, Shackleton House, 4 Battle Bridge Lane,
London SE1 2HX.

Without limiting the author's and publisher's exclusive rights, any unauthorised use of this publication to train generative artificial intelligence (AI) technologies is expressly prohibited. HarperCollins also exercise their rights under Article 4(3) of the Digital Single Market Directive 2019/790 and expressly reserve this publication from the text and data mining exception.

Author: Rebecca Kitchen
Series editor: Alan Parkinson
Publisher: Cathy Martin
Product manager: Roisin Leahy
Development editor and project manager: Lucy Hobbs
Copyeditor: Mike Harman
Proofreader: Sarah Ryan
Cover designer: Gordon MacGilp
Typesetter: Six Red Marbles, India
Production controller: Alhady Ali
Printed and bound n the UK by Martins the Printers

This book contains FSC™ certified paper and other controlled sources to ensure responsible forest management.

For more information visit: www.harpercollins.co.uk/green

collins.co.uk/sustainability

Cambridge International Education material in this publication is reproduced under licence and remains the intellectual property of Cambridge University Press & Assessment.

This text has not been through the endorsement process for the Cambridge Pathway. Any references or materials related to answers, grades, papers or examinations are based on the opinion of the author(s). The Cambridge International Education syllabus or curriculum framework associated assessment guidance material and specimen papers should always be referred to for definitive guidance.

Contents

Geographical skills
1 Geographical skills practise — 5

Physical geography

2.1 Changing river environments
2.1.1 The main characteristics of rivers and drainage basins — 8
2.1.2 The main landforms associated with hydrological processes — 10
2.1.3 Rivers present opportunities and hazards for people — 12
2.1.4 *DSE The Mekong River* — 14
2.1.5 *DSE River pollution in sub-Saharan Africa* — 16

2.2 Changing coastal environments
2.2.1A The physical processes that shape our coastlines — 18
2.2.1B Coastal erosion — 20
2.2.2 Opportunities and hazards for people from coasts — 22
2.2.3 *DSE Cedar Key, Florida, US* — 24
2.2.4 *DSE The Great Barrier Reef Marine Park* — 26

2.3 Changing ecosystems
2.3.1 Characteristics of the Antarctic ecosystem — 28
2.3.2 Threats to the Antarctic ecosystem and how they can be managed — 30
2.3.3 The characteristics of the tropical rainforest ecosystem — 32
2.3.4 Managing main threats to tropical rainforest ecosystems sustainably — 34
2.3.5 *DSE Borneo's tropical rainforest* — 36

2.4 Tectonic hazards
2.4.1 The Earth's structure and distribution of earthquakes and volcanoes — 38
2.4.2 Features associated with earthquakes and volcanoes — 40
2.4.3 The impacts of tectonic hazards — 42
2.4.4 Managing the impacts of tectonic hazards — 44
2.4.5 *DSE The Turkey–Syria earthquake* of 2023 — 46
2.4.6 *DSE Icelandic volcanoes* — 48

2.5 Climate change
2.5.1 The natural and human causes of climate change — 50
2.5.2 Impacts of climate change at a range of geographic scales — 52
2.5.3 Responses to climate change — 54
2.5.4 *DSE Climate change in Iceland* — 56

Human geography

3.1 Changing populations
3.1.1 Populations grow and decline   58
3.1.2 Population structures change over time   60
3.1.3 *DSE China's population policy*   62
3.1.4 The causes and impacts of international migration   64
3.1.5 *DSE International migration in the Philippines and US*   66

3.2 Changing towns and cities
3.2.1 Where people live   68
3.2.2 Opportunities and challenges of urbanisation   70
3.2.3 The management of urban growth   72
3.2.4 *DSE Cairo*   74

3.3 Development
3.3.1 What do we mean by development?   76
3.3.2 What are development indicators?   78
3.3.3 What is sustainable development and how can it be achieved?   80
3.3.4 *DSE Fiji*   82

3.4 Changing economies
3.4.1 Classifying industry   84
3.4.2 The impact of globalisation and the role of transnational corporations   86
3.4.3 *DSE Impacts of globalisation on Costa Rica*   88
3.4.4 The growth of the tourist industry   90
3.4.5 *DSE Tourism in Iceland*   92

3.5 Resource provision
3.5.1 How is our food produced?   94
3.5.2 Investigating the global patterns of food supply and demand   96
3.5.3 The challenges of food supply   98
3.5.4 *DSE Australia's changing food security*   100
3.5.5 How is our energy produced?   102
3.5.6 What are the global patterns of energy supply and demand?   104
3.5.7 The impacts of energy production   106
3.5.8 *DSE Portugal's renewable energy*   108

Answers for all the questions in this Workbook are available from
http://www.collins.co.uk/internationalresources.

1 Geographical skills practise

Use this chart to help record your progress with each of the geographical skills you will need to be able to show you understand. The final column indicates where you can practise each skill in this book and the Student's Book.

Skill	*Needs more work*	*Got it!*	*Places to practice (SB = Student's Book; WB = Workbook; R&P = Review and Practice)*
Cartographic skills			
Select, construct and interpret maps using direction, scale, symbols, a key and other information			SB: 1.1.1, 2.2.3, 2.5.4, 3.3.2 WB: 3.1.5, 3.4.5, 3.5.3
Extract, interpret, analyse and evaluate information presented on maps			SB: 1.1.4, 1.1.5, 1.1.6, 1.1.7, 1.1.8, 2.1.5, 2.1 R&P, 2.2.1, 2.2.2, 2.2 R&P, 2.3.3, 2.3.5, 2.4 R&P, 2.5.2, 3.1.1, 3.2 R&P, 3.3.2, 3.4.4, 3.5.1, 3.5.3, 3.5.6 WB: 2.1.4, 2.2.2, 2.3.3, 2.3.5, 2.5.2, 3.2.1, 3.3.1, 3.3.3, 3.4.2, 3.5.6
Use co-ordinates, latitude and longitude, 4 and 6 figure grid references			SB: 1.1.2, 2.2.1 WB: 2.3.1
Give directions using the 16-point compass and bearings from grid north			SB: 1.1.1, 2.4 R&P WB: 2.4.2, 2.4.4
Measure and estimate distances and area			SB: 1.1.1, 1.2.1 WB: 2.2.1
Use and interpret gradient, contour lines and spot heights; calculate differences in height			SB: 1.1.3 WB: 2.4.2
Interpret cross-sections and transects			SB: 1.1.3, Section 1 R&P, 2.1.1, 2.1 R&P WB: 2.1.2
Graphical skills			
Select, present, construct and communicate data through appropriate graphs, charts and diagrams using relevant scales and annotations to present information			SB: 1.3.1, 1.3.2, 1.3.4, 2.2.4, 2.3.5, 2.3 R&P, 3.1.1, 3.1.2, 3.4.1, 3.5.6 WB: 2.3.2, 2.4.6, 3.1.3

Section 1: Geographical skills | practise

Skill	Needs more work	Got it!	Places to practice (SB = Student's Book; WB = Workbook; R&P = Review and Practice)
Extract, interpret, analyse and evaluate information presented on graphs, charts and diagrams			SB: 1.3.3, 2.3.5, 2.3 R&P, 2.5 R&P, 3.1.1, 3.1.2, 3.1 R&P, 3.4.3, 3.5.6 WB: 2.1.3, 2.2.4, 2.3.1, 2.3.2, 2.3.3, 2.5.1, 3.1.1, 3.1.2, 3.1.3, 3.1.4, 3.4.5, 3.5.4, 3.5.5, 3.5.8
Identify and evaluate variations, trends and patterns from data provided			SB: 1.3.1, 1.3.2, 1.3.3, 1.3.4, 2.3.5, 3.5 R&P WB: 2.2.1, 3.2.4, 3.3.1, 3.3.2
GIS and image skills			
Deconstruct, interpret, analyse and evaluate visual images including photographs (aerial; vertical and oblique and ground level), cartoons, pictures, diagrams, satellite images			SB: 1.4.3, 1.4.4, 2.1.2, 2.1 R&P, 2.2.1, 2.2.2, 2.2 R&P, 2.3.3, 2.3 R&P, 2.4.1, 2.4.2, 2.4 R&P, 2.5.2, 2.5 R&P, 3.2.2, 3.3.1, 3.4.1, 3.4.4, 3.4 R&P, 3.5.1, 3.5.6, 3.5.8 WB: 2.1.1, 2.1.2, 2.1.3, 2.1.5, 2.2.1, 2.2.3, 2.2.4, 2.3.1, 2.3.3, 2.4.2, 2.5.3, 2.5.4, 3.2.2, 3.2.3, 3.5.1, 3.5.6
Analyse written text from a variety of sources for understanding, interpretations and to recognise bias			SB: 3.1.3 WB: 2.3.5, 2.4.6, 2.5.1
Suggest improvements to, issues with, or reasons for using maps, graphs, statistical techniques and visual sources including photographs (aerial; vertical and oblique and ground level) and diagrams			SB: 3.4.1 WB: 3.5.7
Use GIS to identify trends, patterns, issues and solve problems			SB: 1.4.2 WB: 2.2.1, 2.3.4, 2.4.1, 2.4.4, 3.5.2
Recognise the benefits and limitations of using GIS			SB: 1.4.1 WB: 2.1.3
Mathematical skills			
Demonstrate an understanding of number (add, subtract, multiply and divide), area and scale			SB: 1.2.1, 3.1.1, 3.4.5, 3.4. R&P WB: 3.2.1, 2.4.5, 3.1.1
Use standard notation, including positive and negative indices			SB: 1.2.1, 1.2.3, Section 1 R&P WB: 3.1.2
Understand and use significant figures			SB: 1.2.1

Skill	Needs more work	Got it!	Places to practice (SB = Student's Book; WB = Workbook; R&P = Review and Practice)
Understand and use proportion, ratio, magnitude and frequency			SB: 1.2.2, 3.1 R&P WB: 3.1.2
Understand and use mean, mode and median, range, decimals, fractions, percentages and ratios			SB: 1.2.3, 3.4 R&P WB: 3.1.4, 3.2.1
Design fieldwork data collection sheets and collect data with an understanding of accuracy, sample size and procedures, control groups and reliability			SB: 1.2.4, 1.5.1, 1.5.2, Section 1 R&P
Complete, interpret and evaluate tables of data			SB: 2.2.4, 3.1.1, 3.3.1, 3.3.2 WB: 2.4.3, 2.4.5, 2.5.3, 3.3.4
Identify and describe relationships between two or more sets of data			SB: 1.2.4, 3.3.1, 3.4 R&P WB: 3.3.4
Identify and interpret trends or relationships over time and draw line of best fit			SB: 1.3.2, 3.1 R&P, 3.5 R&P WB: 3.3.4, 3.4.1
Make predictions, interpolate and extrapolate trends from data			SB: 3.5 R&P WB: 2.5.2
Identify weaknesses and limitations in statistical presentations of data			SB: 1.2.4
Draw and justify conclusions from numerical and statistical data			SB: 3.1.2, 3.3.1 WB: 3.4.3
Fieldwork skills			
Follow the route to geographical enquiry			SB: 1.5.1, 1.5.2, 1.5.3, 2.1.1 WB: 2.1.1, 2.2.4
Select and use appropriate fieldwork equipment			SB: 1.5.2, 1.5.3, 2.1.1 WB: 2.1.1, 3.4.4
Select and conduct appropriate fieldwork techniques			SB: 1.5.1, 1.5.2, 1.5.3, 2.1.1 WB: 2.1.1, 3.4.4
Devise and use appropriate data collection sheets			SB: 1.5.1, 1.5.2, 1.5.3, 2.1.1
Devise and use risk assessments and be able to work safely whilst out in the field			SB: 1.5.1, 2.1.1

2.1 Changing river environments

2.1.1 The main characteristics of rivers and drainage basins

Student's Book pages 76–8 | Syllabus learning objective 2.1

1 Match the correct term to its definition.

Term	Definition
Overland flow	Some of the precipitation that reaches the ground continues downwards through the soil.
Infiltration	Precipitation falling into the drainage basin can be obstructed by the leaves of trees and by ground vegetation.
Interception	Some of the precipitation reaching the ground flows over the surface until it reaches the river channel.
Percolation	Water moves from the soil down through the pores in the underlying rock on its way to contributing to groundwater flow.

[4]

2 Which process of river erosion would you expect to be strongest in a river that has quite acidic water, and where the banks and bed are made of limestone or chalk? Explain why.

[2]

3 Annotate the photograph below to show some of the characteristics of river deposition.

[3]

Skills link Imagine that you are carrying out some fieldwork to assess how the characteristics of a river change downstream. Suggest how you might measure the width and depth of the river. You can draw a labelled diagram to help you.

....

....

....

....

....

....

[4]

2.1.2 The main landforms associated with hydrological processes

Student's Book pages 79–81 | Syllabus learning objective 2.1

1 Define the following landforms using no more than 10 words for each definition.

Meanders:

Flood plain:

Waterfall:

Oxbow lake:

Pothole: [5]

2 Label the diagram below to identify the key features of a flood plain in the lower course of a river.

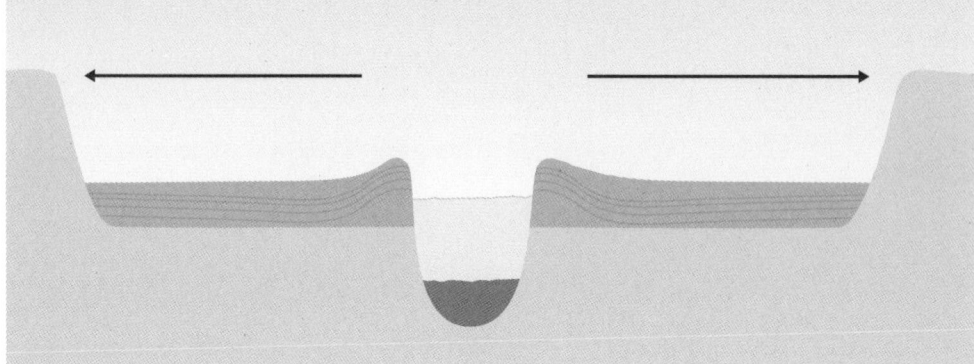

[8]

3 What are rapids? Explain how they are formed.

[3]

Skills link This is an aerial photograph of a river delta in Mozambique. What is the evidence that deposition is happening in this stretch of the river?

....

....

....

.... [2]

2.1.3 Rivers present opportunities and hazards for people

Student's Book pages 82–6 | Syllabus learning objective 2.1

1 State four reasons why early settlers would have wanted to live near rivers.

[4]

2 Look at the photo which shows the Pinheiros River flowing through São Paulo in Brazil. Suggest two opportunities and two challenges that the river might present for the people that live here.

Opportunities:

Challenges:

[4]

Section 2: Physical geography | 2.1 Changing river environments

3 Your task is to protect a small village around 1 km² in size from river flooding. The budget for this is $1 million. You can select one or more of the hard and soft engineering strategies in the table. Which would you choose to protect the village? Explain why.

Strategy	Cost
Dams and reservoirs	$1 million per dam/reservoir
Human-made levees	$500 000 per 100 metres
Dredging	$500 000 per 100 metres
Flood relief channels	$750 000 per channel
Afforestation	$200 000 per km²
Contour ploughing	$100 000 per km²
Terracing	$250 000 per km²
Land-use zoning	$100 000 per km²

[6]

Skills link The Rivers Trust produces a map which shows an annual summary of sewage discharges into rivers in England and Wales. It uses proportional circles to display information about the number of events in each region. Why are the proportional circles an effective way of displaying these data?

[1]

2.1.4 DSE The Mekong River

Student's Book pages 87–8 | Syllabus learning objective 2.1

1 Name the six countries that the Mekong River passes through.

[6]

2 Complete the following sentences to explain the issues from flooding in the Mekong River Basin.

- Flooding in the Lower Mekong Basin is threatening

- Flood risks are minimised by

- The Xe Namnoy flood event of July 2018 caused

[3]

3 The Mekong River Basin has problems linked to flooding, but it is important to be optimistic about the future. Suggest two reasons to be hopeful about the future of the Mekong River.

Section 2: Physical geography | 2.1 Changing river environments

....

.... [2]

Skills link Look at the information below and answer the following questions. You can also explore river catchments online using GIS, for example the Schools Atlas of World Rivers.

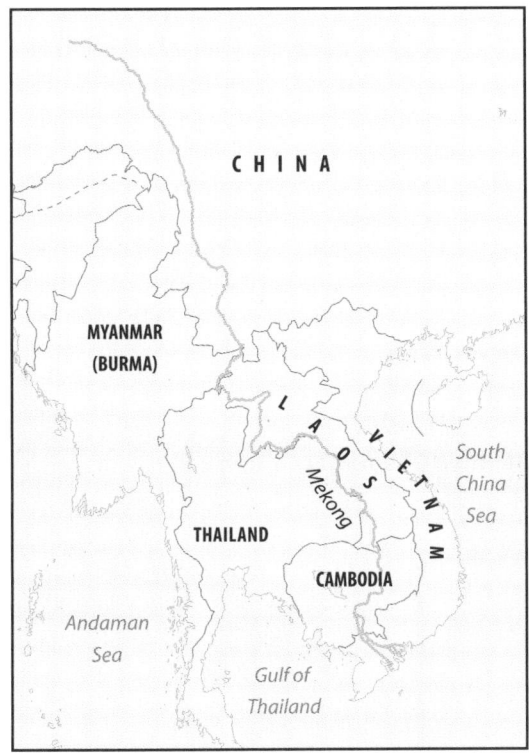

Mekong River
Main channel length: 4 900 km
Catchment area: 802 000 square km
Average discharge: 480 cubed km
Total channel length in catchment: 8 800 km

- How long is the total channel length in the catchment?

  .... [1]

- How large is the river's catchment area?

  .... [1]

- What is the river's average discharge?

  .... [1]

- Which country is the Mekong delta in?

  .... [1]

15

2.1.5 DSE River pollution in sub-Saharan Africa

Student's Book pages 89–91 | Syllabus learning objective 2.1

1 Why have 30% of countries in sub-Saharan Africa experienced a decline in their water quality in the last 20 years?

....

....

....

.... [2]

2 Draw five images to illustrate why Kenya is experiencing a pollution crisis. Use the captions to guide you.

Pesticides and fertilisers flow into rivers from agricultural areas.

Pollutants from coal and other mining operations flow into rivers.

Rivers in urban areas are full of plastics, detergents, disinfectants, human effluent and petrochemicals. These affect rivers, but also pollute soils and underground aquifers.

Pollutants flowing into Lake Victoria have led to the growth of water hyacinth – an invasive species from South America – which takes over local vegetation.

Sewage systems cannot cope with the high levels of pollution and contamination in the rivers. Often, open sewage lines carry microbial pathogens, which cause diseases, into rivers.

[5]

3 Imagine that you were in charge of improving water quality in Kenya. What actions would you take and why? Suggest at least three things that you would do.

1. ....

2. ....

3. ....

[6]

2.2 Changing coastal environments

2.2.1A The physical processes that shape our coastlines

Student's Book pages 98–100 | Syllabus learning objective 2.2

1 There are two different types of waves, destructive and constructive. Look at the characteristics below and circle which type of wave they are describing.

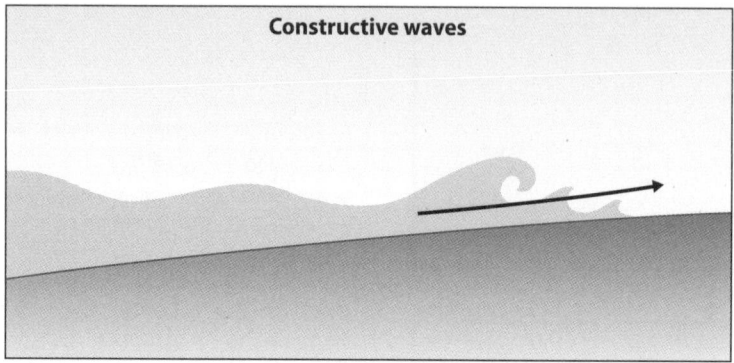

Swash is stronger than backwash, so waves run gently up the beach – material is carried onto the beach and deposited there.

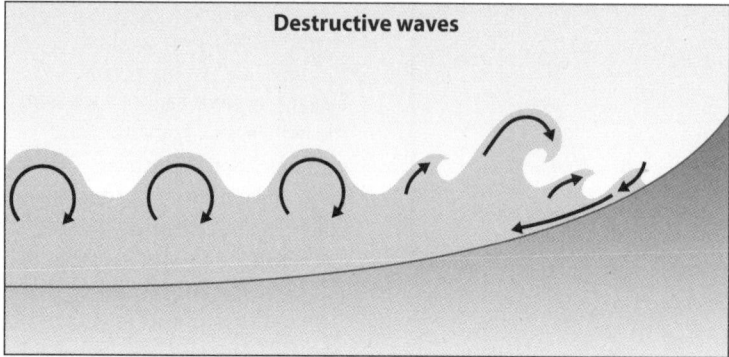

Backwash is stronger than swash, so waves crash onto the beach – material is eroded from the coastline.

1. Waves are close together <constructive / destructive>
2. Creates gently sloping beaches <constructive / destructive>
3. The swash is stronger than the backwash <constructive / destructive>
4. Material is eroded from the coastline <constructive / destructive>

[4]

2 Annotate the diagram below to explain the process of longshore drift.

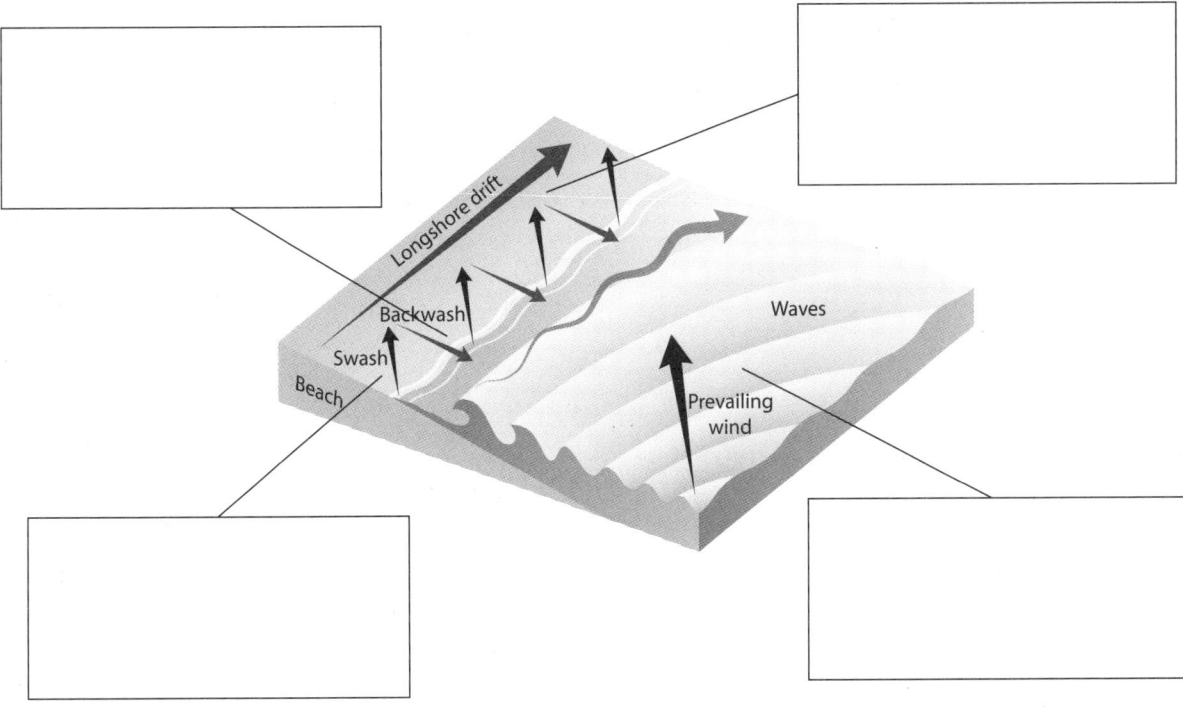

[4]

3 Waves tend to deposit their sediment load in sheltered bays or where the coastline changes direction. Why do you think this happens?

[2]

Skills link Using an atlas, measure the distance from the northeast coast in Brazil to Land's End in the UK. Explain why Land's End often experiences strong, powerful wave conditions.

[3]

Section 2: Physical geography | 2.2 Changing coastal environments

2.2.1B Coastal erosion

Student's Book pages 100–6 | Syllabus learning objective 2.2

1 State three factors which affect the rate of coastal erosion at a discordant coastline.

1. ....

2. ....

3. .... [3]

2 Put the following statements in the correct order to explain how a spit is formed. Add an order number next to each box.

| The energy of the waves decreases, allowing sediment to accumulate and form a narrow ridge extending into the sea. | ☐ |

| Behind the spit, a sheltered area is created where wave energy is reduced. Sediment accumulates here and can lead to the formation of habitats such as mudflats or salt marshes, which are rich in biodiversity. | ☐ |

| Longshore drift transports sediment along the coastline until it reaches a point where the coastline changes direction, such as at a headland or river mouth. | ☐ |

| The end of the spit can be curved as changes in wind direction shape the deposited sand and pebbles. | ☐ |

| The spit will continue to grow as long as sediment is deposited faster than it is eroded by waves. However, it can become unstable due to storm surges or changes in tidal patterns that might lead to erosion or breaching of the spit. | ☐ |

[5]

3 What do you think this coastline will look like in 100 years? Add labels and explain why you think these changes might happen.

[4]

Skills link Measure the rate of erosion along this coastline by comparing the two maps.

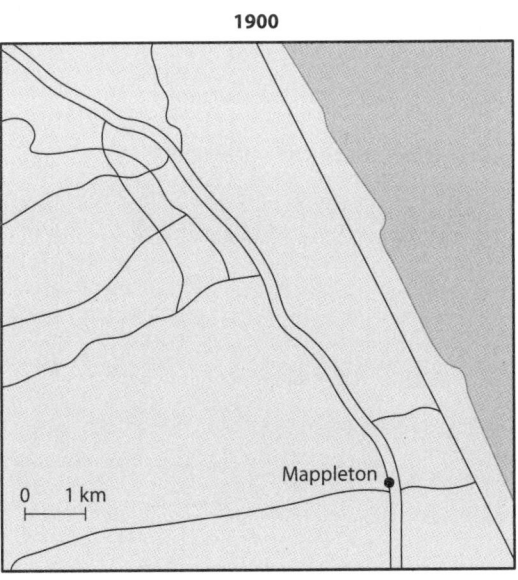

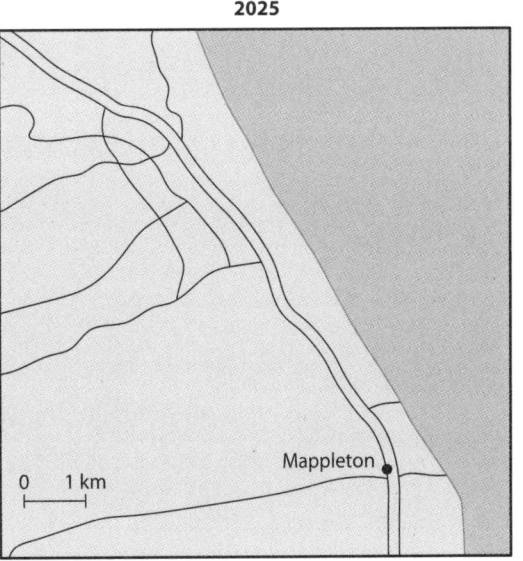

[2]

Section 2: Physical geography | 2.2 Changing coastal environments

2.2.2 Opportunities and hazards for people from coasts

Student's Book pages 107–16 | Syllabus learning objective 2.2

1 Suggest two ways in which this stretch of coastline has been managed.

[2]

2 Using the flow chart below, explain the effects of nutrient pollution on coral reefs.

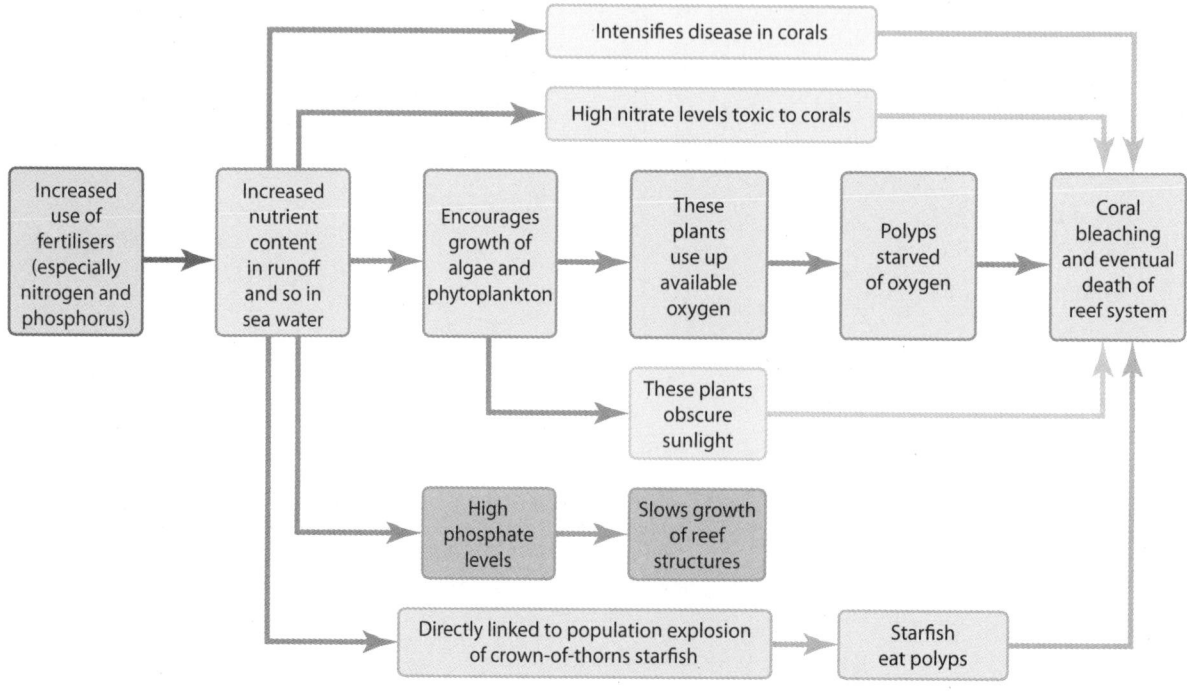

[6]

3 Explain how mangrove swamps protect the coast.

[4]

Skills link Look at the satellite map of Bangladesh and the surrounding regions. Explain why Bangladesh is one of the countries most likely to be flooded.

[3]

2.2.3 DSE Cedar Key, Florida, US

Student's Book pages 116–9 | Syllabus learning objective 2.2

1 Why do you think that people are attracted to live in Cedar Key, Florida?

You could have a virtual walk around the area on Google Streetview to help you answer this question.

[3]

2 Why is Cedar Key susceptible to being flooded?

[3]

3 Explain why the Living Shorelines project was a success.

[6]

Skills link Take a careful look at the photo of storm damage in Cedar Key. Then complete the layers of inference questions below, starting at the centre of the grid.

What else would I like to find out? What other questions do I need to ask?

> What does the photograph not tell me?
>
> > What can I infer from the photograph? What guesses can I make?
> >
> > > What does the photograph definitely tell me?

[4]

2.2.4 DSE The Great Barrier Reef Marine Park

Student's Book pages 119–22 | Syllabus learning objective 2.2

1 Why do you think two million tourists visit the Great Barrier Reef each year?

[3]

2 A nonsense word has been included in each of the following reef management strategies. Highlight the word and suggest a suitable replacement.

- Rangers educate hippos on how their trips affect the reef.

- Fines of up to US$1 million can be forced on cupboards for polluting.

- Tourist hairdryers are not allowed to stop in sensitive areas.

- Jellyfish patrol the area checking up on illegal activity. [4]

3 What questions would you like to ask about the Great Barrier Reef and its management? Write five questions using the question grid below to provide your question starters.

	is	did	can	would	will	might
Who						
What						
Where						
Why						
When						
How						

[5]

Skills link Look at the bar graph below which shows the change in sea surface temperature of the Great Barrier Reef. Describe the pattern shown. What impacts might this have on the reef?

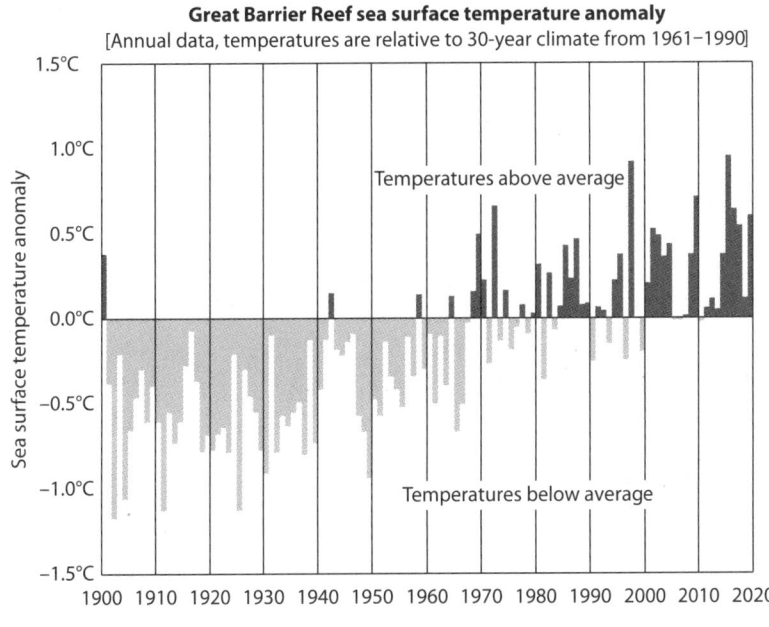

[6]

2.3 Changing ecosystems

2.3.1 Characteristics of the Antarctic ecosystem

Student's Book pages 128–32 | Syllabus learning objective 2.3

1 Why are there no land mammals, no trees and no shrubs in Antarctica?

[3]

2 Using the diagram below, explain how the angle of the Sun in the sky affects the temperature in Antarctica.

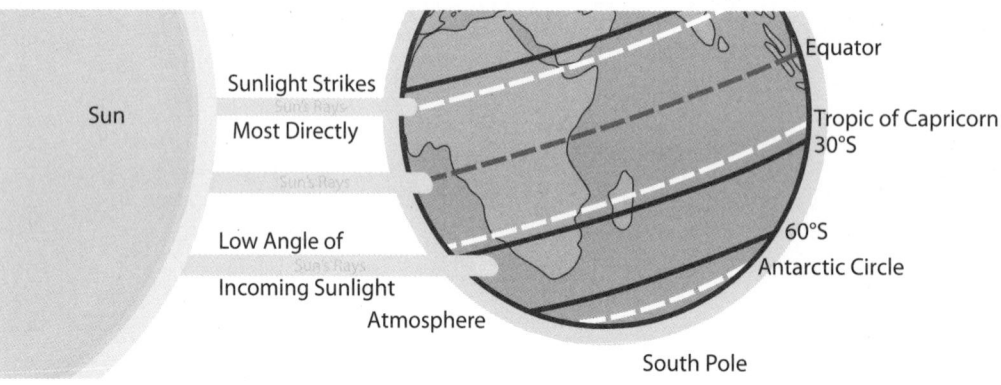

[4]

3 Suggest which species might exist at each stage of the Antarctic food chain below.

Primary Producer	Primary Consumer	Secondary Consumer	Tertiary Consumer
Phytoplankton			

[3]

Skills link Look at the climate graph for Vostok Station in Antarctica below and answer the following questions.

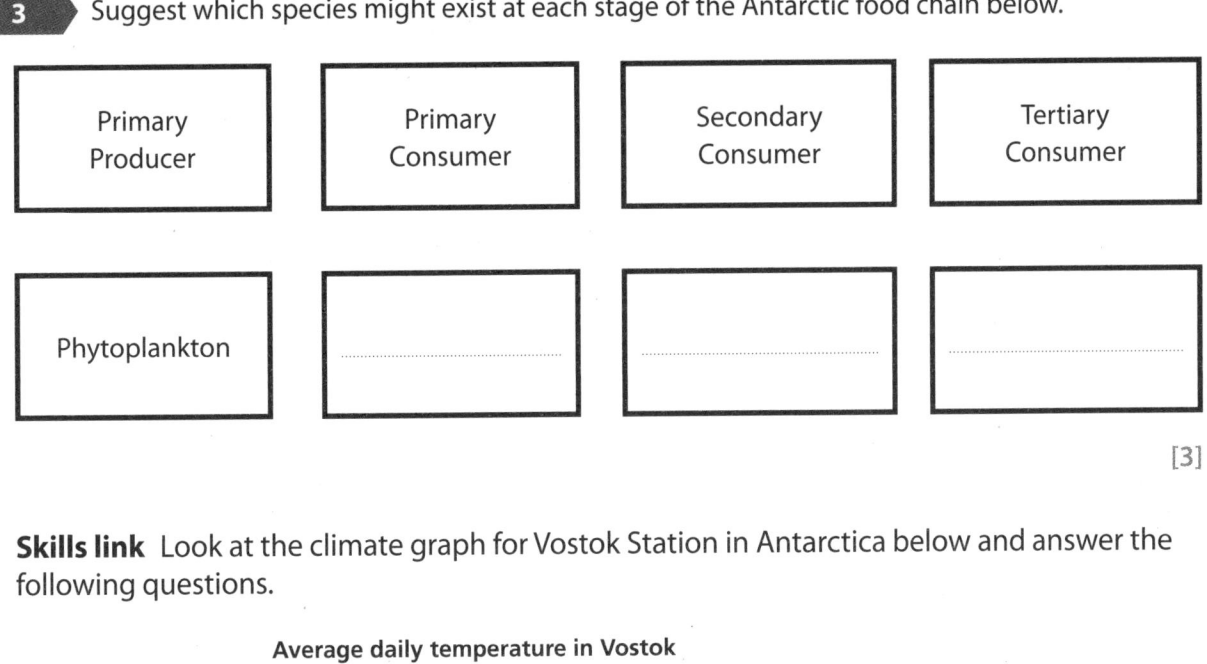

- In which two months are temperatures the warmest? .... [2]

- How warm are these months? .... [1]

- Which month is the coldest month? .... [1]

- How cold is it? .... [1]

- What is the temperature range for Vostok? .... [1]

2.3.2 Threats to the Antarctic ecosystem and how they can be managed

Student's Book pages 133–36 | Syllabus learning objective 2.3

1 ▶ Antarctica was closed to tourists during the COVID-19 pandemic. There were only 15 tourists in the 2020/21 season and 100 000 during the 2022/23 season, of which 70 000 set foot on the continent. Sketch a suitable graph to show these data in the space below.

[4]

2 ▶ For each of the following impacts, explain how they could damage the Antarctic ecosystem.

- warming of the oceans

....

- bird flu in penguin colonies

....

- sea ice decline

....

[3]

3 What would you suggest should be included in a code of conduct for tourists who are visiting Antarctica? Suggest three things that would be in your code.

....

....

....

.... [3]

Skills link Look at the graph which shows the annual sea ice extent measured in million km².

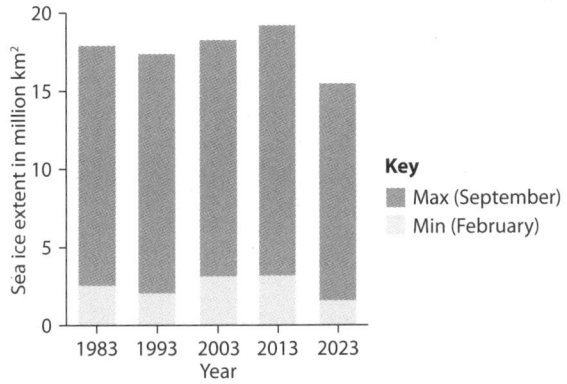

- What was the maximum sea ice extent in 1983?

.... [1]

- What was the minimum sea ice extent in 1983?

.... [1]

- What was the maximum sea ice extent in 2023?

.... [1]

- What was the minimum sea ice extent in 2023?

.... [1]

2.3.3 The characteristics of the tropical rainforest ecosystem

Student's Book pages 136–40 | Syllabus learning objective 2.3

1 Label three parts of the world that have an equatorial climate on the map below.

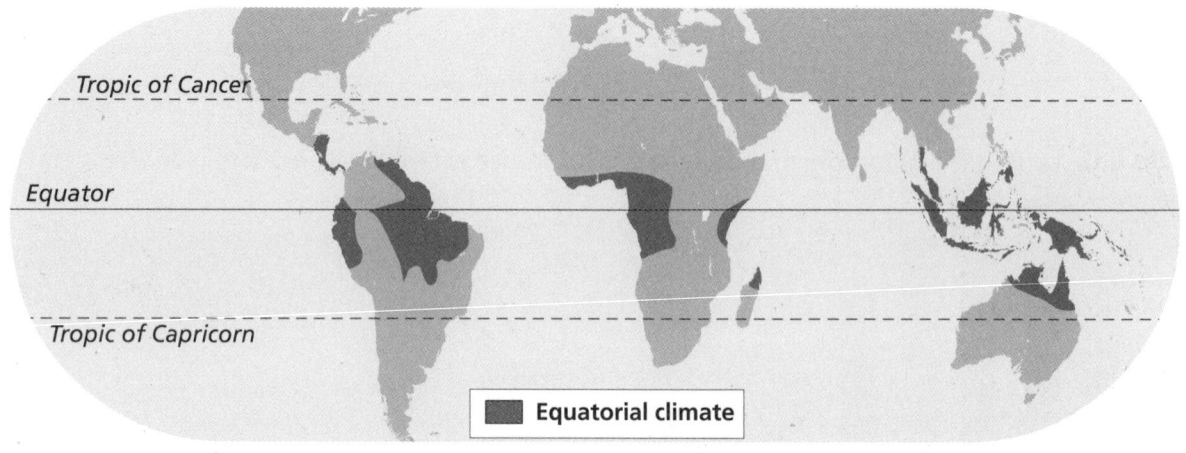

[3]

2 Using the diagram below, explain why tropical rainforest soils are relatively infertile.

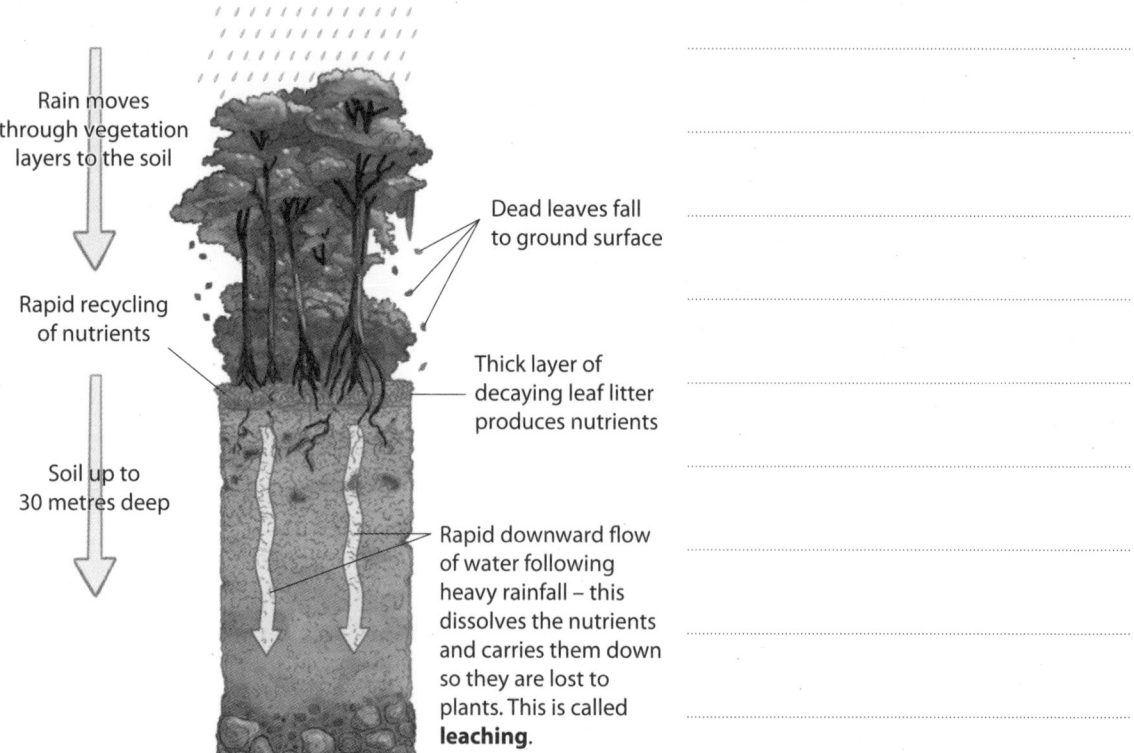

[3]

3 Imagine that you are to visit a tropical rainforest. What five things would you pack to make sure that you are prepared for the environment? Add a label and a brief explanation for each one to the rucksack to explain why.

[5]

Skills link Look at the climate graph for the city of Manaus in the Amazon rainforest and answer the following questions:

- Which month has the most rainfall?

    .... [1]

- How much rainfall is there in this month?

    .... [1]

- Which month has the lowest rainfall?

    .... [1]

- How much rainfall is there in this month?

    .... [1]

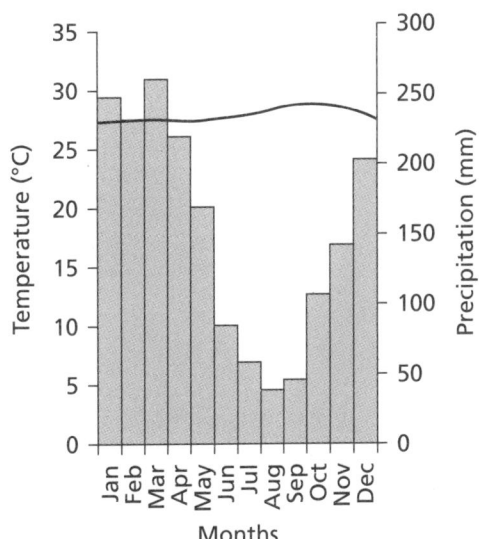

- What phrase describes the pattern of temperature?

    .... [1]

Section 2: Physical geography | 2.3 Changing ecosystems

2.3.4 Managing main threats to tropical rainforest ecosystems sustainably

Student's Book pages 141–4 | Syllabus learning objective 2.3

1 Rearrange these letters to find three of the main threats to the tropical rainforest.

- curtail urge

  ....

- powdery hero

  ....

- carts furniture

  ....

[3]

2 Look at the following impacts of deforestation. For each, state whether it is an economic, social or environmental impact.

Export of forest goods from mining	Increased sedimentation of rivers, increasing risk of flooding	Displacement of Indigenous communities
Competing interests over forest resources can lead to conflict	An increase in jobs in mining, agriculture and hydropower	Increased landslide risk leading to damaged roads and infrastructure

[6]

3 Suggest four things that governments and non-governmental organisations can do to manage tropical rainforests.

1. ....

2. ....

3. ....

4. ....

[4]

Skills link Look carefully at the satellite images below which show the area around Yurimaguas in the Peruvian Amazon in 2001 (left) and 2019 (right). Briefly describe what has happened.

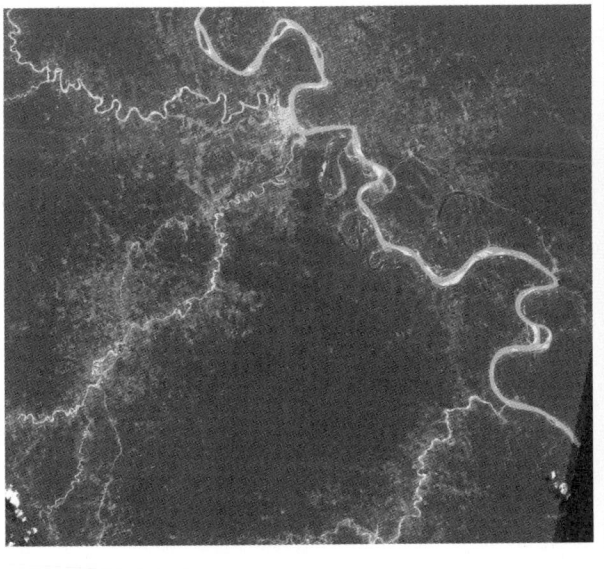
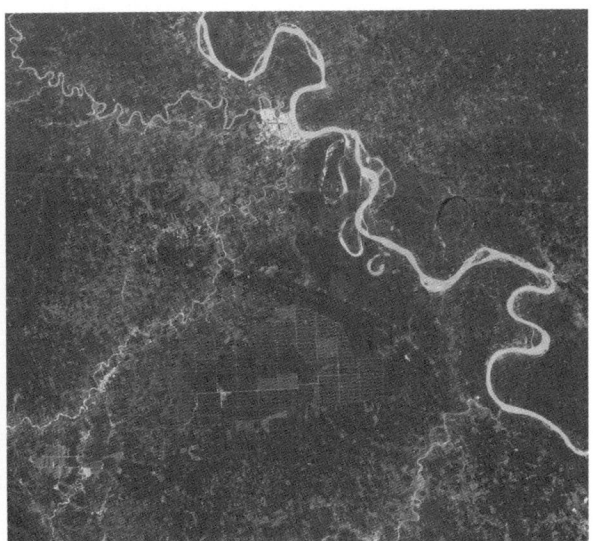

[3]

2.3.5 DSE Borneo's tropical rainforest

Student's Book pages 145–7 | Syllabus learning objective 2.3

1 State three products that have palm oil as an ingredient.

1.

2.

3.

[3]

2 Look at the maps below which show the decline of Borneo's forests between 1950 and 2020. Describe how the pattern of rainforest coverage has changed over time.

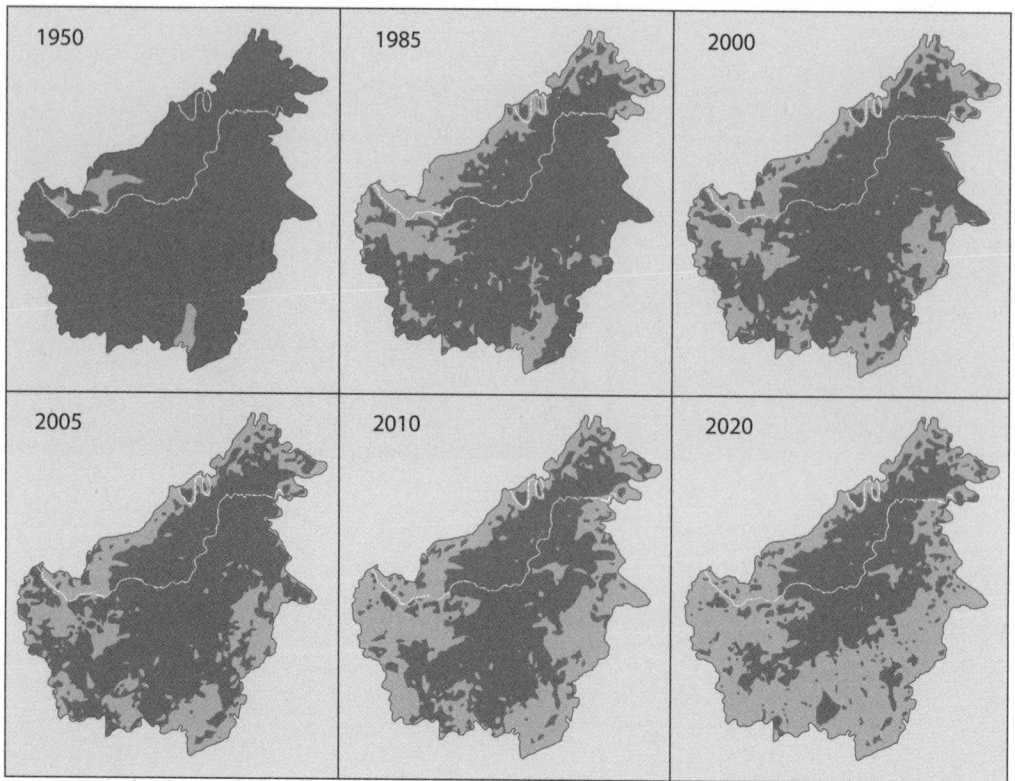

....

....

....

.... [3]

3 The rate of deforestation in Borneo has slowed down in recent years. Suggest three reasons why this might be the case.

1. ....

....

2. ....

....

3. ....

.... [3]

Skills link Research deforestation in Borneo and describe and summarise the main causes and impacts.

....

....

....

....

....

....

....

....

.... [6]

2.4 Tectonic hazards

2.4.1 The Earth's structure and distribution of earthquakes and volcanoes

Student's Book pages 154–7 | Syllabus learning objective 2.4

1 The structure of the Earth is composed of several layers – the inner and outer core, the mantle and the crust. State two facts about the mantle.

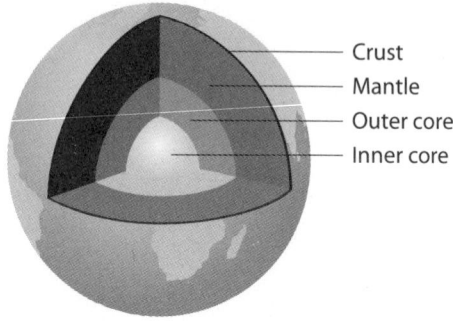

1. ....
....

2. ....
.... [2]

2 Complete the sentences about the Earth's tectonic plates using words from the list. Each word can be used once, more than once or not at all.

| magma | nine | enormous | lithosphere | oceanic |

| crust | continental | boundaries | tectonics |

The Earth's crust is broken up into .... tectonic plates which are constantly moving. The edges of these plates are known as .... and around 90% of all volcanoes and earthquakes occur here. There are two different types of crust. .... crust is dense, relatively thin and is constantly being destroyed and replaced. It sinks underneath the .... crust which is less dense, thicker and cannot be destroyed.

[4]

3 The Hunga Tonga-Hunga Ha'apai volcano erupted explosively on January 15, 2022 in the South Pacific Ocean. This eruption occurred at a destructive plate boundary where the Pacific Plate is subducting beneath the Indo-Australian Plate. Use the diagram to explain why a volcano occurred here.

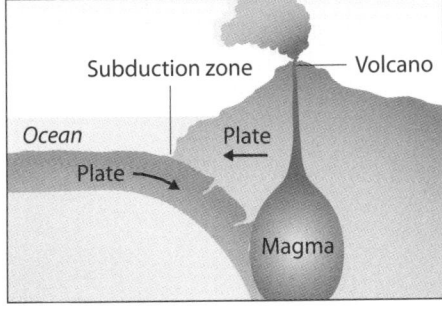

[5]

Section 2: Physical geography | 2.4 Tectonic hazards

2.4.2 Features associated with earthquakes and volcanoes

Student's Book pages 157–9 | Syllabus learning objective 2.4

1 Draw a diagram to show the characteristics of an earthquake in the space below. Make sure you label clearly the focus, the epicentre and seismic waves.

[4]

2 Annotate this photograph to describe the volcanic hazards shown at **A** and **B**.

A. ....

....

....

B. ....

....

....

[2]

3 What type of volcano do you think this is? Explain your answer.

....

....

....

.... [3]

Skills link Look closely at the map below which shows the extent of the Mauna Loa eruption in 2022.

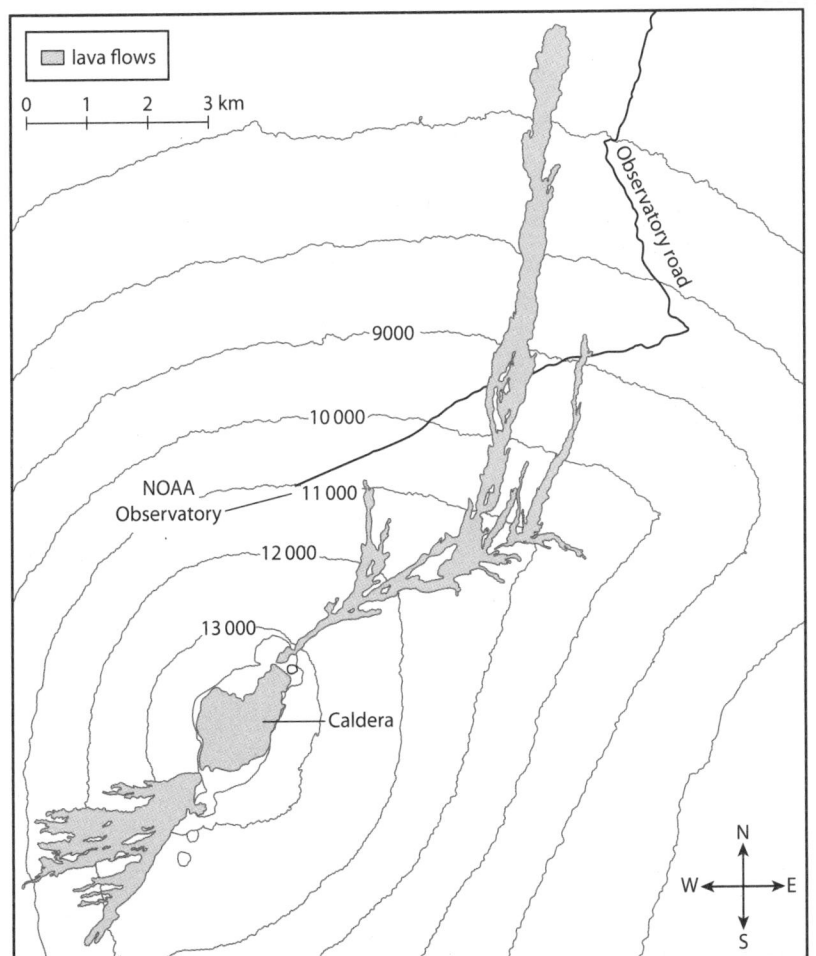

- How high is the crater of Mauna Loa? .... [1]

- In which directions did the lava flow? .... [2]

- How far did the longest lava flow travel? .... [1]

2.4.3 The impacts of tectonic hazards

Student's Book pages 159–61 | Syllabus learning objective 2.4

1 Tick which of the following statements is true:

People live near volcanoes because:

a. the land is fertile ☐

b. geothermal heat can be used to produce electricity ☐

c. they bring water to the surface so that it is easily accessible ☐

d. they bring tourist activity and associated employment. ☐

[1]

2 Earthquakes and, to a lesser extent, volcanoes regularly make the news. Have a look at a recent event of this type to see how people were affected – this could become your detailed specific example for this unit. Where did the event occur? How were people affected? Why do you think they were affected in this way? Write some notes or create a mind map in the space below.

[6]

3 Japan is a wealthy country and used to earthquake activity. However, the 2011 Tohoku earthquake was devastating, killing 18 000 and displacing over 200 000. Give three reasons why the impacts of this earthquake were so great.

1. ....

   ....

2. ....

   ....

3. ....

   ....
   [3]

Skills link Look at the data table, which shows Moment Magnitude and Mercalli Scale readings for five recent earthquakes:

Earthquake	Moment Magnitude Scale	Mercalli Scale
2011 Tohoku earthquake	9.0	X
2023 Turkey-Syria earthquake	7.8	X
2021 Haiti earthquake	7.2	VII to IX
2015 Nepal earthquake	7.8	VIII to IX
2016 Kumamoto earthquake	7.0	IX

What are two conclusions that you can draw from this data?

....

....

....

....
[2]

2.4.4 Managing the impacts of tectonic hazards

Student's Book pages 162–3 | Syllabus learning objective 2.4

1 What is the instrument in the picture below? What does it measure?

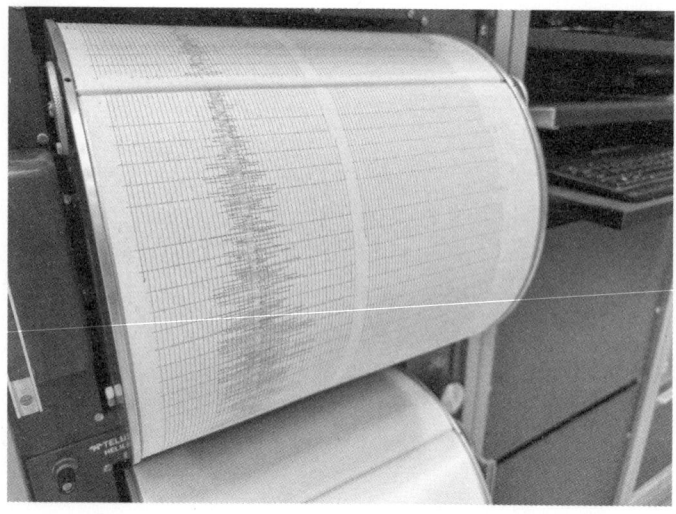

....

....

.... [2]

2 Suggest three strategies that can be used to manage the impact of earthquakes and volcanoes.

1.

....

2.

....

3.

.... [3]

Section 2: Physical geography | 2.4 Tectonic hazards

3 ▸ The impacts of tectonic hazards tend to be greater in lower income countries (LICs) than they are in higher income countries (HICs). Why do you think this is?

....
....
....
....
....
.... [4]

Skills link Look at the map, which shows how the eruption of La Cumbre Vieja in September 2021 was managed.

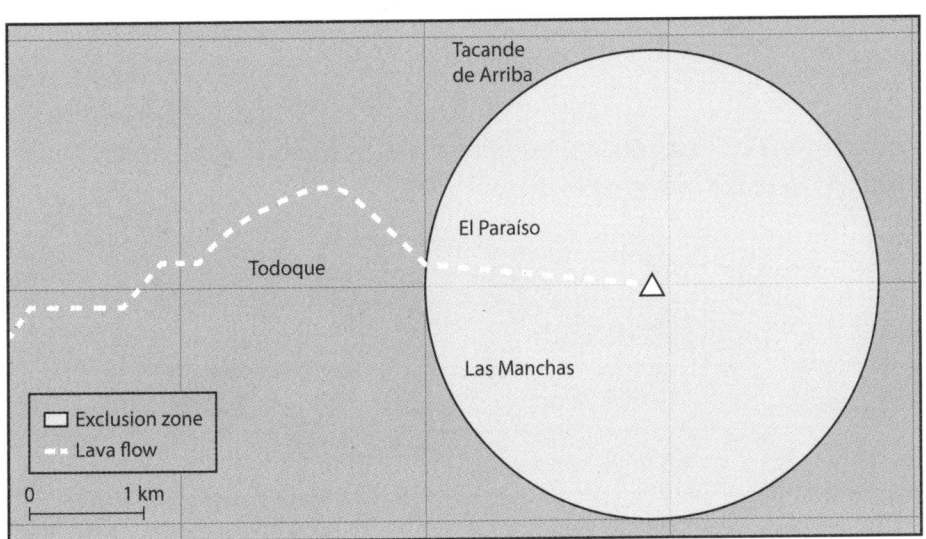

1. How large was the exclusion zone? .... [1]

2. Name one of the villages in the exclusion zone. .... [1]

3. In which direction was the lava flowing or tracing? .... [1]

2.4.5 DSE The Turkey–Syria earthquake of 2023

Student's Book pages 164–5 | Syllabus learning objective 2.4

1 Suggest three reasons why the Turkey-Syria earthquake was so devastating.

1. ....
   ....

2. ....
   ....

3. ....
   ....
   [3]

2 Higher or lower? There are lots of facts and figures that you need to learn for the Turkey-Syria detailed specific example. Here is a reminder of these:

Impact	Turkey	Syria
Number of people killed	57 000 people	5 900 people
Number of people injured	115 000 people	14 500 people
Number of people made homeless	1.5 million people	265 000 people
Number of buildings destroyed	325 000 buildings	10 600 buildings
Total damage estimate	$34 billion (4% of GDP)	$5 billion (56% of GDP)

For each fact in the list below, write down the correct figure and whether it is higher or lower than the one before it.

1. Number of people injured in Turkey: ....

2. Number of schools destroyed in Syria: ....

3. Number of deaths in Syria: ....

4. Number of buildings destroyed in Turkey: .... [4]

3 Complete the sentences about the longer-term impacts of the Turkey-Syria earthquake using words from the list. Each word can be used once, more than once or not at all.

World Health Organisation   300 million   World Vision   years

months   international   health   18 million

There was a significant .... response to the earthquake from governments and non-governmental organisations such as .... In the aftermath it was estimated that .... people in the two countries had been affected and only one in seven .... centres were in operation. Six .... after the earthquake, the Red Cross still had 2500 staff and volunteers working in Turkey supporting the population by providing hot meals and medical support.

[5]

Skills link Refer to the table in question 2 which shows the impacts of the earthquake on both Turkey and Syria. Then answer the questions that follow.

1. How many people were made homeless in total? .... [1]

2. What was the total damage estimate? .... [1]

3. Which country was most impacted by the earthquake? Justify your answer.

....

....

....

[2]

2.4.6 DSE Icelandic volcanoes

Student's Book pages 166–7 | Syllabus learning objective 2.4

1 Use the diagram below to explain why Iceland is one of the most volcanically active places in the world.

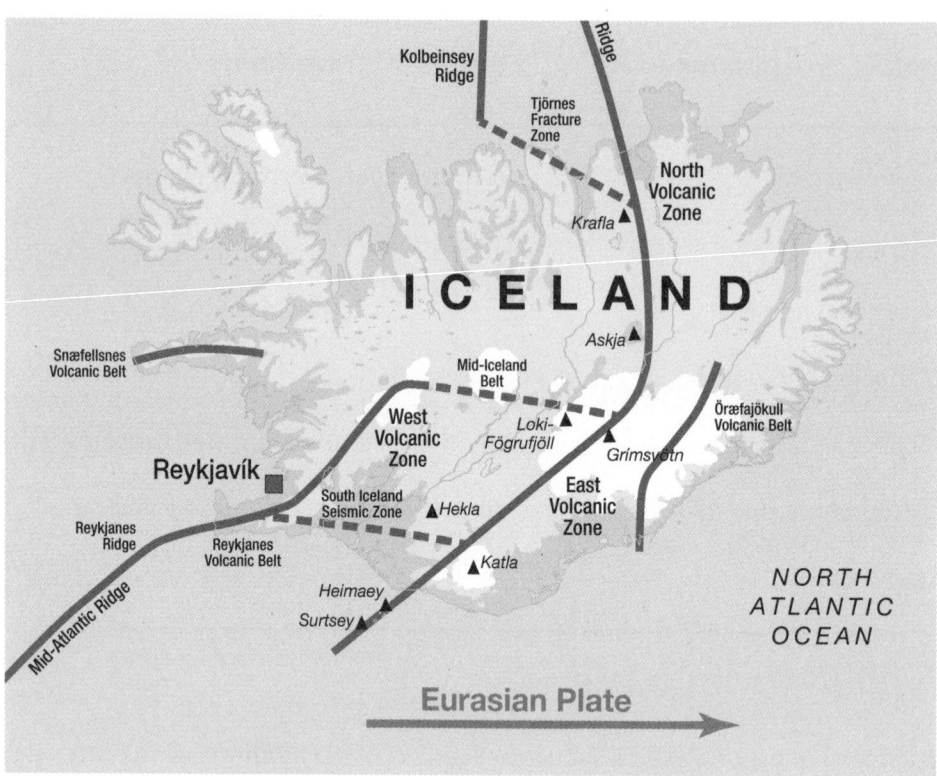

[3]

2 Match the danger posed from Icelandic volcanoes with their impact.

Volcanoes located underneath glaciers	can cause respiratory problems
Chemicals deposited during eruptions	can cause floods
Gas emissions from volcanoes	can poison crops and livestock
Ash clouds	can disrupt air transport

[4]

3 Below is a photograph of Geldingadalir volcano on the Reykjanes peninsula which erupted in May 2021. Annotate the photo to explain the opportunities posed by Iceland's volcanoes.

[2]

49

2.5 Climate change

2.5.1 The natural and human causes of climate change

Student's Book pages 174–7 | Syllabus learning objective 2.5

1 Match each greenhouse gas with a source.

| carbon dioxide | methane | nitrous oxide |

| cattle farming | agricultural fertilisers | burning fossil fuels |

[3]

2 True for who? Look at the potential effects of climate change in the diagram below. For three of the effects, suggest who is likely to be most affected and who is likely to be least affected.

THE EFFECTS OF CLIMATE CHANGE

- Rising sea temperatures will mean the oceans expand, leading to an average worldwide sea-level rise of 40 cm by 2100 – this would mean widespread flooding of low-lying areas.
- Melting polar ice caps, ice sheets (in countries like Greenland) and glaciers could cause a sea-level rise of up to 5 metres – a severe problem for the 40 per cent of the world's population who live close to the coast.
- There could be changes in extreme weather events – e.g. temperatures over 40 °C causing wildfires in Australia, more hurricanes in the Caribbean, deadly heatwaves in Europe and floods in Egypt.
- Wars may be fought as the global population grows and precious resources such as food and water become scarce in some countries.
- Changes to farming as equatorial areas become too hot and tropical crops are grown further north.
- The coral reefs that provide many countries (including Belize, Australia and the Maldives) with a big tourist attraction could die.
- Tropical diseases become more widespread – malaria, for instance, could become common in Europe.
- Extinction of wildlife that is unable to adapt to the changing climate – some scientists estimate up to one-third of all species could become extinct over the next 100 years.

[6]

3 'There is no evidence of climate change.' Use the information in the Student Book and your own knowledge to prove that this statement is not true.

[6]

Skills link Use the acronym TEA (Trend, Examples, Anomalies) to describe the graph below which shows how the temperature has increased between 1880 and 2020.

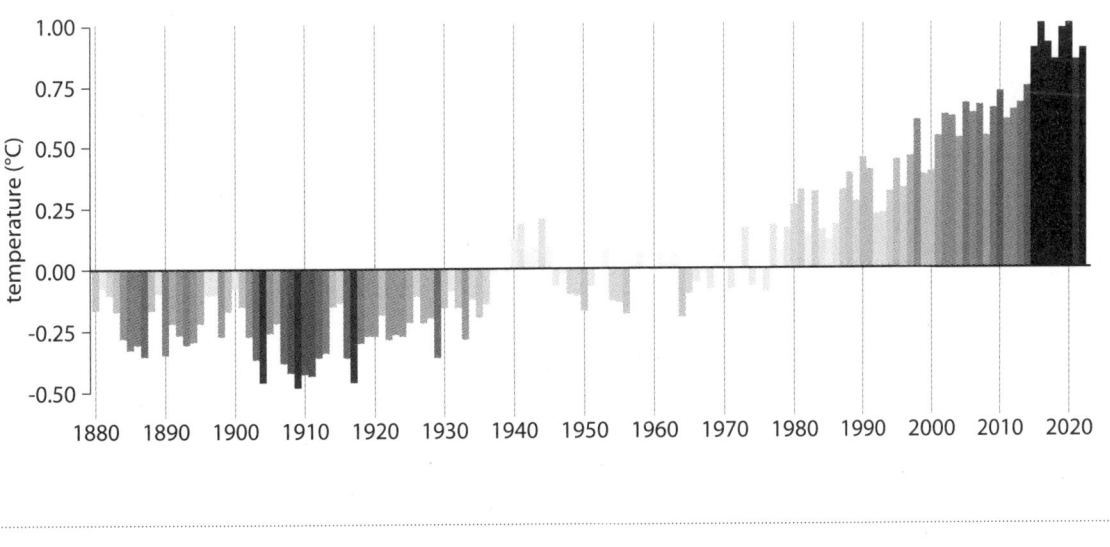

Global temperature increase compared to 1951–1980 average

[3]

2.5.2 The impacts of climate change at a range of geographic scales

Student's Book pages 177–9 | Syllabus learning objective 2.5

1 We can look at the impacts of climate change using a range of geographic scales. For each of the following scales, explain what they mean.

global

national

local

individual [4]

2 Migrants from the Carteret Islands in the South Pacific (origin) were evacuated to Bougainville off the coast of Papua New Guinea (destination) in 2009. What might be two impacts of this migration on the origin and two impacts on the destination? You might want to look at 3.1 Changing populations in the Student's Book to help you.

Impacts on the Carteret Islands (origin)

Impact on Bougainville (destination)

[4]

3 Look at the following impacts of climate change. Decide whether they are global, national or local impacts and suggest why you have classified them in this way.

- sea levels rise

Section 2: Physical geography | 2.5 Climate change

- people migrate due to sea level rise

- there is flooding in fields that grow crops

- coral reefs bleach and die

- changes in extreme weather events

[5]

Skills link Climate change is likely to create 170 million internal climate migrants per region by 2050. Look at the map below and answer the following questions:

- Which region is likely to see the highest total number of migrants?

- Which region is likely to see the highest number of migrants as a proportion of its population?

- How many migrants are there likely to be in total?

- What percentage of the world's population is this? [4]

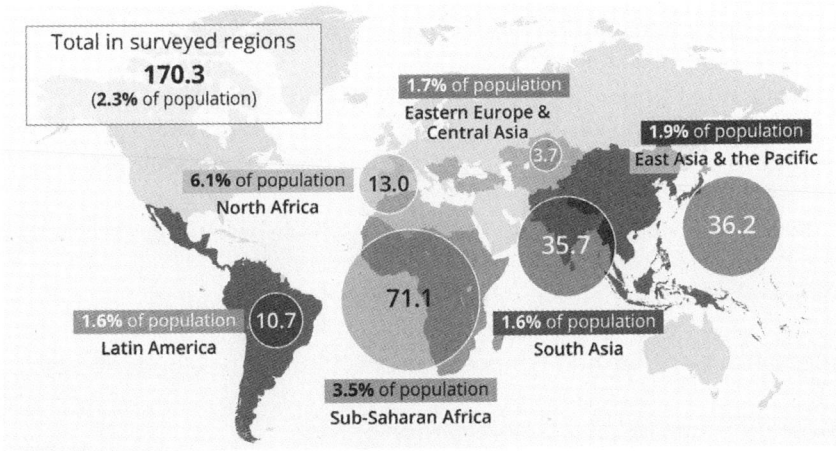

53

Section 2: Physical geography | 2.5 Climate change

2.5.3 Responses to climate change

Student's Book pages 179–82 | Syllabus learning objective 2.5

1 Complete the table with the key information about the following climate change agreements.

Agreement	Year	Main outcome(s)
The Kyoto Protocol		
The Marrakesh Agreement		
The Paris Agreement		

[6]

2 A student has written a paragraph about the technological solutions to climate change, but they have missed out the examples. Complete the paragraph by inserting the correct example from the following choices:

- climate geoengineering
- alternative feed for cattle
- carbon capture and storage
- encouraging home working
- alternative protein sources

[5]

There are potentially technological solutions which could halt climate change. .... would reduce emissions from transport to work and heating office buildings. .... is where carbon dioxide gases are removed from the atmosphere and stored elsewhere, often under the ground or the seabed. Cattle farming is a major source of methane and so people can eat .... or providing an .... such as seaweed may reduce cattle's methane emissions by up to 80%. Finally, there are various different ideas which come under the heading .... These include refreezing the poles by brightening the clouds above them and greening the oceans with algae to absorb more carbon dioxide.

Using the information in the table below, explain how the United Kingdom has adapted to climate change.

Adaptations	Mitigations – national	Mitigations – individuals
Improving flood defences such as the Thames Flood Barrier	Carbon capture systems such as Net Zero Teesside	Encouraging life-style changes and reducing energy use
Enforcing building regulations which take account of extreme weather conditions	Green technology investment	Buying energy-efficient lightbulbs and household appliances
Introducing action plans for extreme cold weather and heatwaves	Household subsidies for heat Pumps to replace inefficient fossil fuel boilers	Installing home insulation and double / triple glazing
Building sea defences and combatting coastal erosion	Planting new forests	Installing solar panels
Working with water companies to reduce wasted water	Development of sustainable power for aircraft	Encouraging people to buy local food and to shop local
	Tax incentives and funding for people to buy electric cars	
	Research into hydrogen-based fuels	

[6]

2.5.4 DSE Climate change in Iceland

Student's Book pages 182–5 | Syllabus learning objective 5.4

1 This is Siggi, who owns a fishing boat in Iceland. What are three of the impacts of climate change that might be affecting him now and in the near future?

....

....

....

....

....

.... [3]

2 State four other effects of climate change in Iceland that Siggi has not discussed in Question 1.

....

....

....

.... [4]

3 Use all the knowledge that you have gained in this chapter to create an action plan for Iceland. Suggest three actions you would take for Iceland to adapt effectively to climate change and explain why these would be your priorities.

Priority 1 ....

....

Priority 2 ....

....

Priority 3 ....

.... [6]

Skills link Look at the four labels below and mark an appropriate place for each one on the graph.

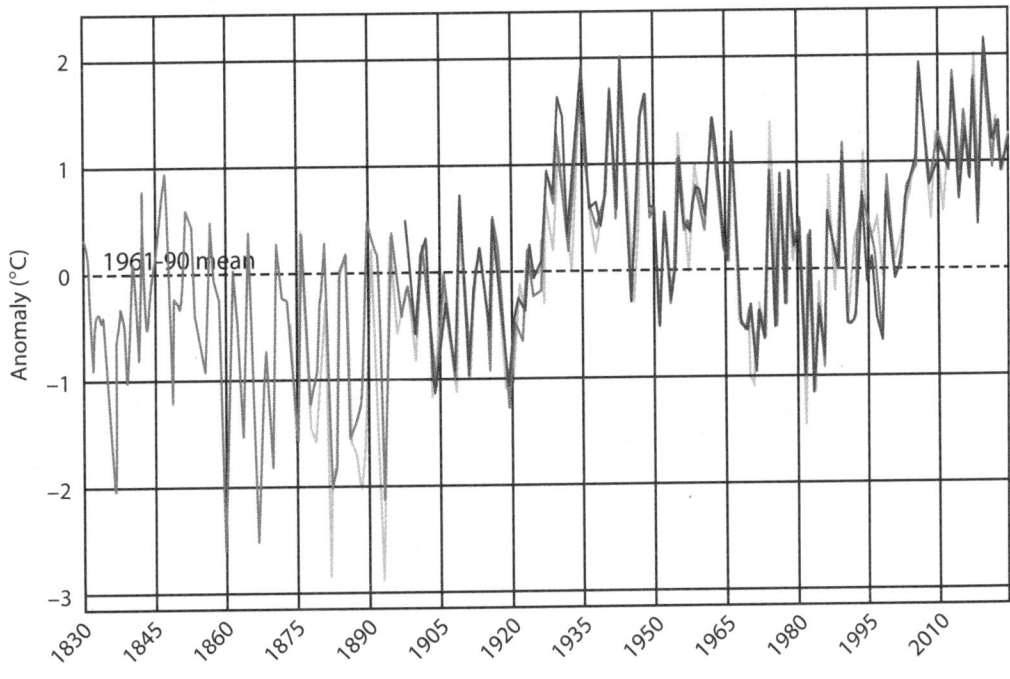

Station
— Stykkisholm
— Telgarhom
— Bolungarvik

- The temperature is 3 °C below the 1961–90 mean.
- The temperature is 2 °C above the 1961–90 mean.
- The temperature is about the same as the 1961–90 mean.
- The temperature is 1 °C above the 1961–90 mean.

[4]

3.1 Changing populations

3.1.1 Populations grow and decline

Student's Book pages 192–203 | Syllabus learning objective 3.1

1 What key terms do these statements describe?

- The increase in population size that occurs when live births are greater than deaths over the course of a year. Birth rate – death rate = positive number

- The decrease in population size that occurs when live births are less than deaths over the course of a year. Birth rate – death rate = negative number

- The number of infant deaths per 1000 live births. [3]

2 Look at the map. What is the net migration rate in the country that you live in? Does your country have more immigrants than emigrants or more emigrants than immigrants?

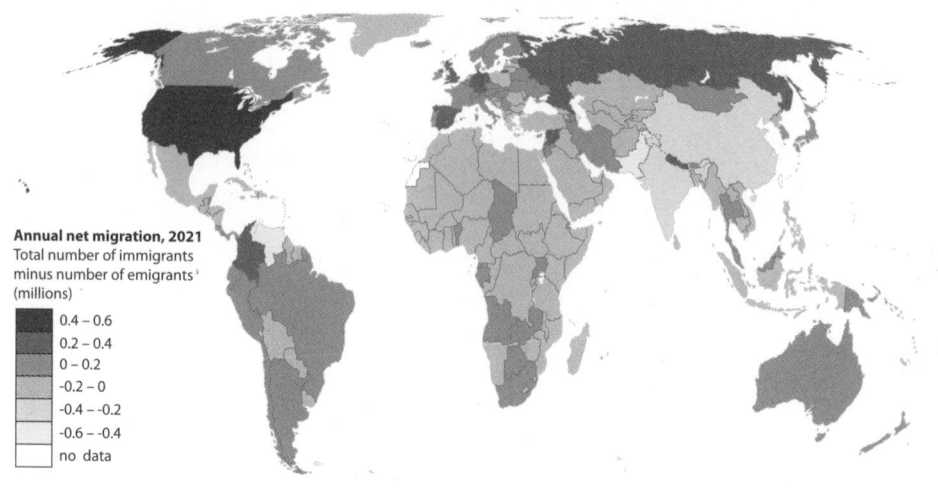

Annual net migration, 2021
Total number of immigrants minus number of emigrants (millions)
- 0.4 – 0.6
- 0.2 – 0.4
- 0 – 0.2
- -0.2 – 0
- -0.4 – -0.2
- -0.6 – -0.4
- no data

[4]

Skills link Which stage of the Demographic Transition Model (DTM) is being described in each sentence below?

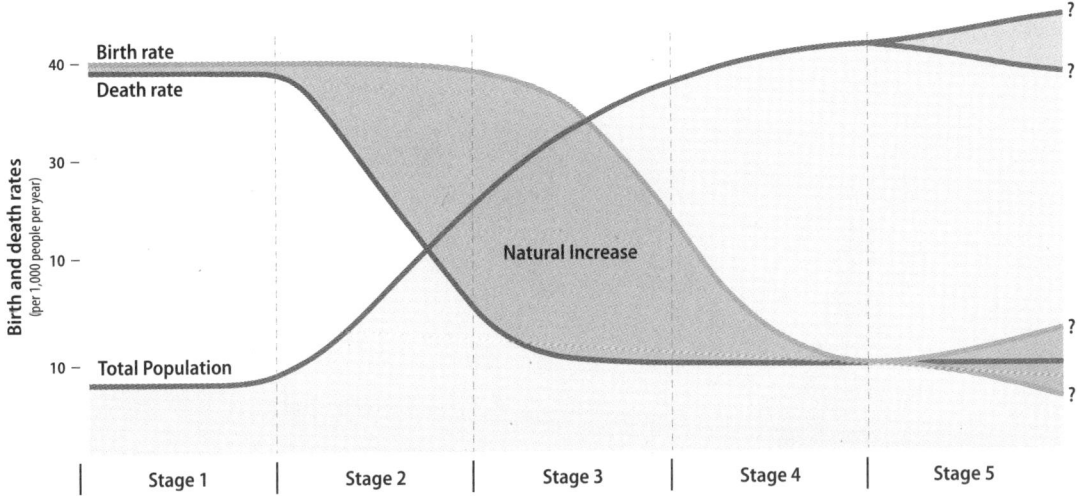

- The birth rate and death rate are both falling but the death rate is falling more slowly. Therefore, while the population is still increasing, the rate of increase has slowed.

- The birth and death rates are both high. This means that the total population is relatively stable or is increasing slowly.

- The birth rate and death rate are both low. The population starts to fall but then becomes stable.

- The birth rate is high, but the death rate is falling rapidly. This leads to a rapid increase in the total population.

[4]

3.1.2 Population structures change over time

Student's Book pages 203–11 | Syllabus learning objective 3.1

1 Take a close look at the population pyramid for Bangladesh in 2024. What information does a population pyramid present?

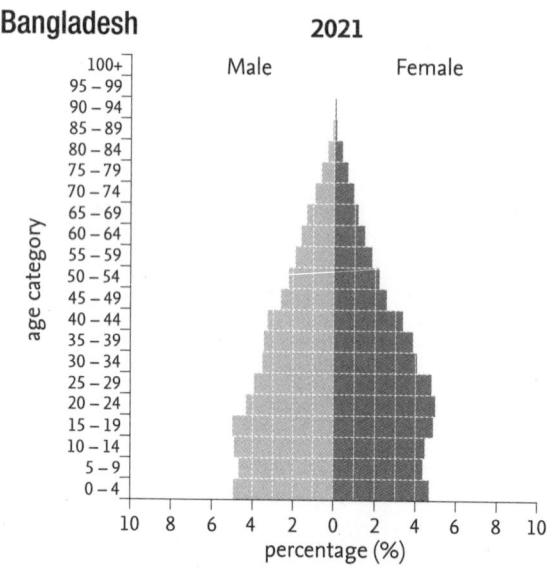

[3]

2 What does the shape of the population pyramid tell you about the population structure of this country?

[4]

Section 3: Human geography | 3.1 Changing populations

3 Use the following equation to calculate the dependency ratio for Bangladesh.

$$\text{Dependency ratio} = \frac{\text{Number of dependents or non-working age group}}{\text{Population aged between 15 to 64 years}}$$

You will need to use the population pyramid from Question 1 to help you. What does this tell you about whether this country has a youthful or an ageing population?

....

....

....

....

....

[4]

Skills link See if you can find a population pyramid for your country. Sketch its shape and annotate its key features in the space below.

[4]

3.1.3 DSE China's population policy

Student's Book pages 212–14 | Syllabus learning objective 3.1

1 Are the following statements about China's population policy true or false?

- By the 1970s, China's population growth was rapid. ....

- The one-child policy was more successful in rural areas than it was in cities. ....

- The two-child policy was announced in 2015. ....

- China has a very balanced population structure – there are roughly the same number of men as there are women. ....

- One of the impacts is that there is an increased dependency ratio. .... [5]

2 This is China's population pyramid in 2023. Annotate the pyramid to explain why its population structure is 'unbalanced'.

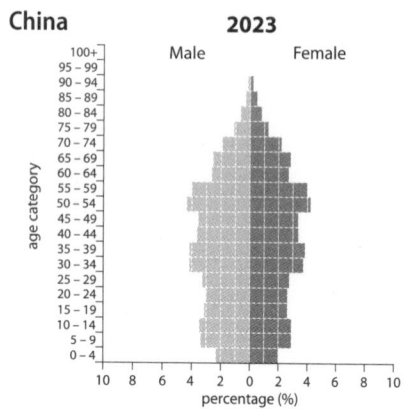

[4]

3 Do you think that China's one-child policy was a success? Explain why you think this.

....

....

....

....

....

.... [6]

Skills link What would be an appropriate type of graph to present the information in the table below? Why do you think it would be effective? Sketch the graph in the box below.

10-year period between population census years	% population change in China	% population change in Asia	% population change in the world
1970–1980	20.0	23.7	20.5
1980–1990	14.8	22.0	19.6
1990–2000	10.8	15.7	15.2
2000–2010	5.8	12.1	12.9
2010–2015	2.5	5.4	6.5

....

....

....

[4]

3.1.4 The causes and impacts of international migration

Student's Book pages 214–22 | Syllabus learning objective 3.1

1 Match the correct key term to the definition. One of the four terms will not match.

refugee   **irregular immigrant**   **asylum seeker**   **economic migrant**

Many people migrate to find a better life for themselves and their families. They often send remittances back to their families. ....

People who are forced to leave their country to escape war, persecution or a natural disaster have the right to be protected by international law. ....

These are migrants who want to be recognised as refugees but who are still waiting for their status to be confirmed. ....

[3]

2 Describe how points-based migration systems work. Suggest one reason why they might be a useful way of managing international migration and one problem that they can cause.

[4]

3 Suggest four impacts of migrants on the origin country and four impacts on the destination country.

Origin country which may be war torn

Destination country which may need to expand its workforce

Impacts on the origin country:

....

....

....

.... [4]

Impacts on the destination country:

....

....

....

.... [4]

3.1.5 DSE International migration in the Philippines and US

Student's Book pages 222–5 | Syllabus learning objective 3.1

1 Migration in numbers. Describe what these different figures indicate in the detailed specific example on migration from the Philippines to the US.

- $38 billion: ....

- $3500: ....

- $200: ....

- 51%: ....

- 10%: .... [5]

2 The population pyramid for the Philippines in 2020 is shown below. How can you tell that its population is youthful?

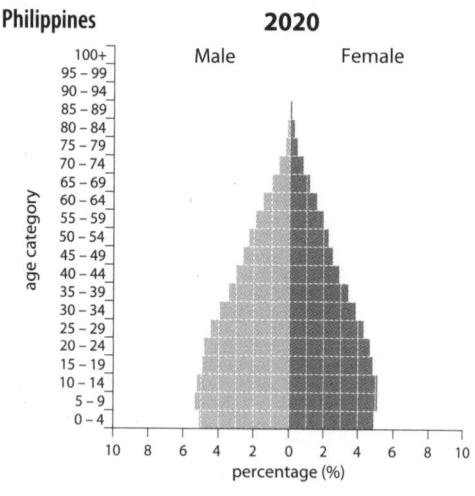

....

....

.... [3]

Section 3: Human geography | 3.1 Changing populations

3 Would you want to migrate from the Philippines to the US? Explain your answer.

[4]

Skills link Locate the US and the Philippines on the map below. What might be an appropriate way of presenting the flow of international migrants on the map?

[3]

3.2 Changing towns and cities

3.2.1 Where people live

Student's Book pages 232–4 | Syllabus learning objective 3.2

1 What is a megacity? What is the world's largest megacity?

....

.... [2]

2 Look at the map, which shows percentages of people living in urban areas. Then match each of the following percentages to the correct country.

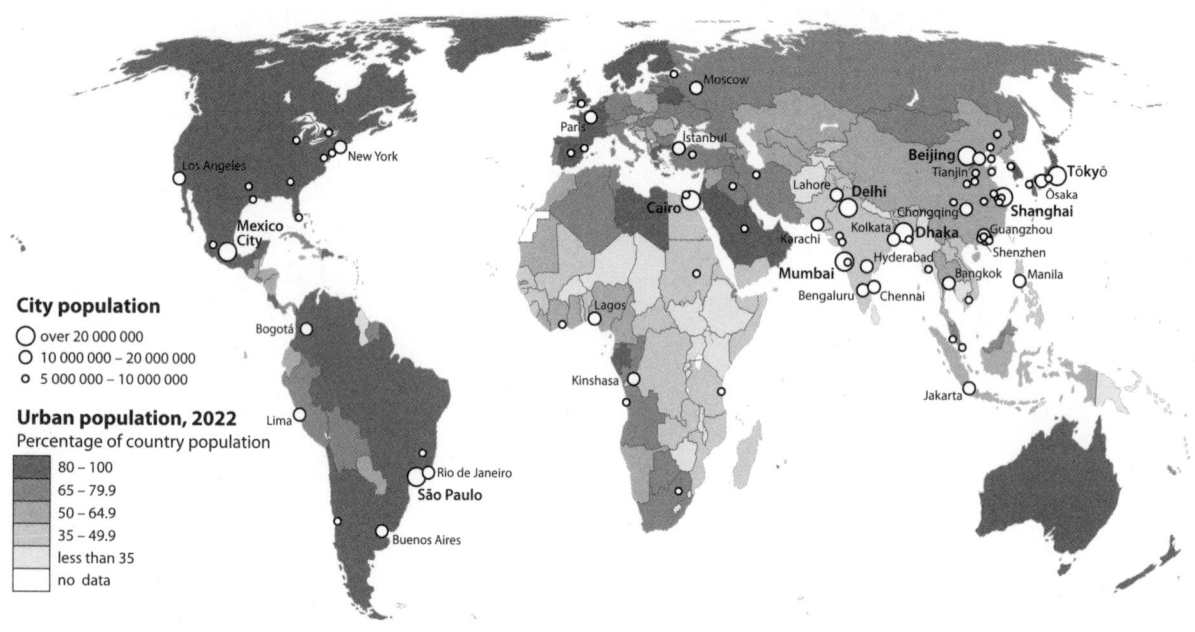

China   India

Australia   Niger

17% ....   64% ....

36% ....   86% .... [4]

3 Look at the table which shows some of the social, economic, environmental and political reasons why people migrate from rural areas to urban areas. Use this information to suggest **four** pull factors encouraging people to move to cities.

Social	Economic	Environmental	Political
• Lack of basic services including healthcare, education, electricity and piped water.	• Extreme poverty because of low standard of living. • Limited access to employment.	• **Soil erosion** – the land has been over cultivated, leading to deforestation. Farmland has become unproductive and degraded. • Low productivity farming – many farms are too small to support families.	• Ongoing conflicts or violence can force people to flee rural areas in search of safety in more stable urban areas. • Personal freedoms – movement to big cities is partly driven by greater opportunities compared to rural regions.

[4]

Skills link Describe the global distribution of megacities shown on the map in question 2.

[3]

3.2.2 Opportunities and challenges of urbanisation

Student's Book pages 235–40 | Syllabus learning objective 3.2

1 What is upward social mobility?

[1]

2 Give **three** examples of jobs which could be described as 'informal'.

[3]

3 Suggest some of the opportunities that living in a large city can provide for its population.

[6]

Skills link Annotate the photograph to highlight some of the problems for people who live in informal settlements. [4]

3.2.3 The management of urban growth

Student's Book pages 241–5 | Syllabus learning objective 3.2

1 Using the diagram, explain what sustainability means? Give an example of how this applies to a city.

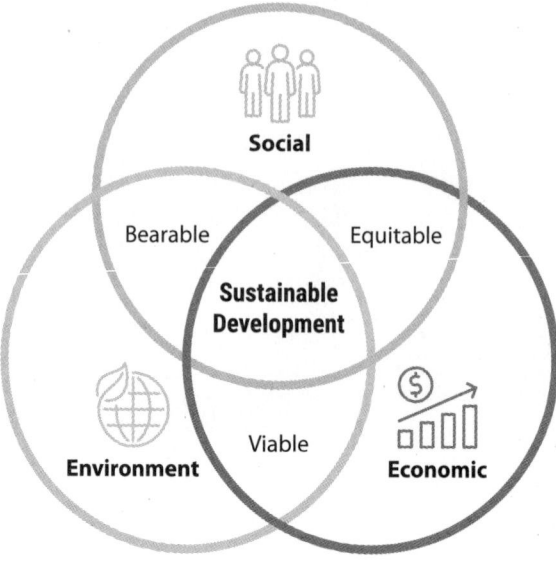

....

....

....

.... [3]

2 Select **two** of the targets for sustainable communities shown in the diagram. How challenging do you think each one will be to achieve? Explain why you think this.

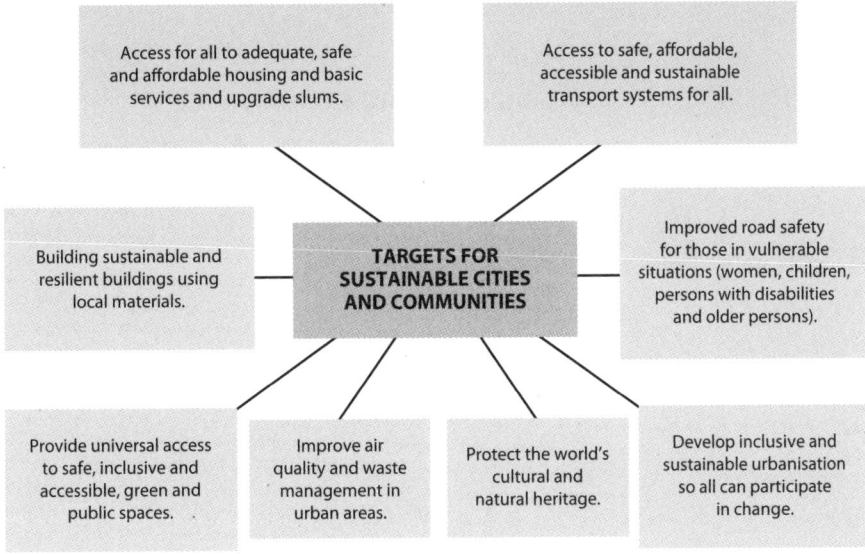

[4]

3 Sketch a design for a sustainable neighbourhood in the box below. Annotate it to show some of its sustainable features.

[10]

Section 3: Human geography | 3.2 Changing towns and cities

3.2.4 DSE Cairo

Student's Book pages 246–51 | Syllabus learning objective 3.2

1 Mark the location of Cairo on the map of the River Nile.

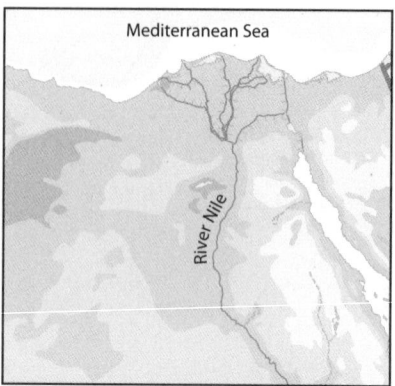

[1]

2 The table shows the challenges of urban sprawl in Cairo. For each challenge, suggest a sustainable strategy that Cairo is using to tackle it. [4]

Challenge	Description	Strategy
Traffic congestion	It has been estimated that Cairo's traffic congestion costs the economy $8 billion a year due to lost productivity and increased fuel consumption.	
Development of informal housing	Historic informal housing has developed in the areas of Ezbet el-Nakhl and Dar El-Salam which are under-served urban residential areas.	
Loss of green spaces	Air pollution levels in Cairo often exceed health standards, with particulate matter (PM10) levels around 120 μg/m³, significantly higher than the recommended maximum of 50 μg/m³.	
Pressure on infrastructure	Rapid urban expansion has outpaced the development of essential infrastructure like roads, water, and sewage systems.	

3 What lessons could your nearest town or city learn from Cairo's sustainability strategies to make it more sustainable?

....

....

....

....

....

.... [4]

Skills link Look at the population growth graph for Cairo. For each date, estimate Cairo's population.

Population growth in Cairo 1950–2024

1950 .... 1970 ....

2000 .... 2020 .... [4]

3.3 Development

3.3.1 What do we mean by development?

Student's Book pages 258–60 | Syllabus learning objective 3.3

1 How would you define a 'good life'? Write **five** features that you would include in a definition.

1. ....

2. ....

3. ....

4. ....

5. .... [5]

2 Describe the pattern of income variation in the UK shown on the map.

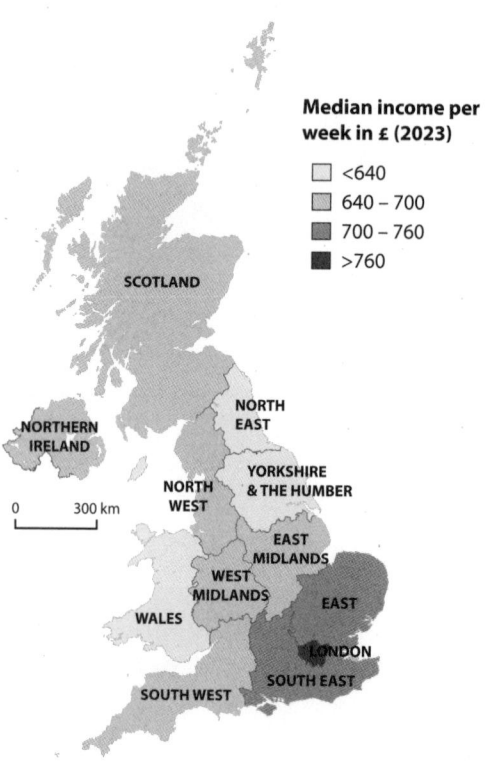

....

....

....

.... [3]

Skills link Look at the scatter graph, which shows the Human Development Index (HDI) data and GDP per capita data from the World Bank in 2022. What word would you use to describe the relationship between HDI and GDP per capita? Explain what this means and provide an example from the graph?

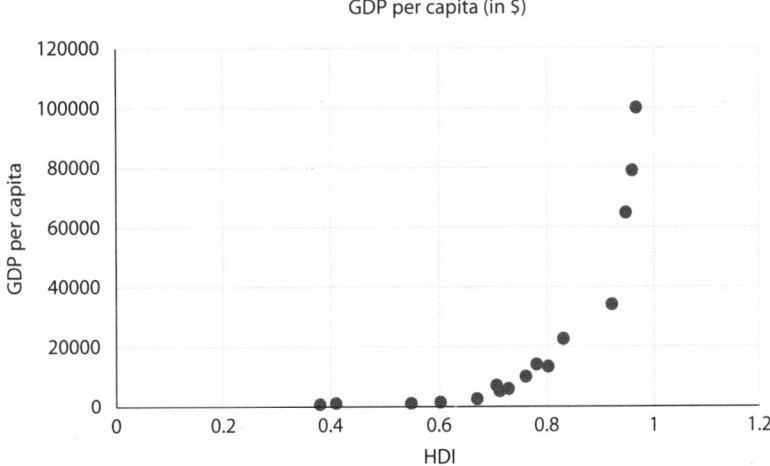

....

....

....

.... [3]

3.3.2 What are development indicators?

Student's Book pages 260–4 | Syllabus learning objective 3.3

1 Give **one** reason why calorie intake might be a useful indicator to measure development and **one** reason why it might be problematic.

[4]

2 Suggest **four** factors that might affect a country's level of development.

[4]

3 Think about this statement: '…any classification of countries by income is not ideal.' Why do geographers classify countries into LICs, MICs and HICs?

....

....

[4]

Skills link This sketch graph shows how the relationship between GDP per capita and life expectancy changes over time for Saudi Arabia.

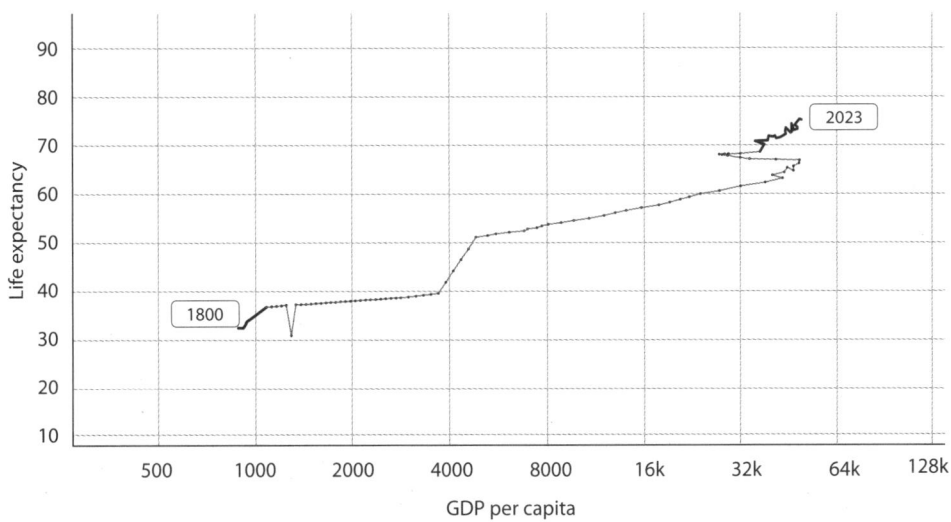

Describe what has happened to the relationship between GDP per capita and life expectancy in Saudi Arabia over time?

....

....

....

....

....

....

[6]

3.3.3 What is sustainable development and how can it be achieved?

Student's Book pages 264–8 | Syllabus learning objective 3.3

1 Suggest **three** strategies for sustainable development.

[3]

2 Complete the following sentences to explain how trade has had an impact on uneven development between countries.

- Global trade favours

- Colonialism has been a major factor

- Even today some companies

- Globalisation and the steady growth in the size of container ships…

[4]

3 How successful do you think debt relief has been in reducing uneven development? Provide reasons to support your view.

[6]

Skills link Look at the map below, which shows the amount of international aid received per capita by different countries. Describe the pattern shown.

Aid received
US$ per person
- 100 – 3214
- 25.6 – 99.9 — average
- 0 – 25.5
- no data
- Donors

Aid received
Official development assistance received in US$ per person. World average US$ 25.6. Statistics are for 2021.

[4]

3.3.4 DSE Fiji

Student's Book pages 269–71 | Syllabus learning objective 3.3

1 What are the two main industries in Fiji?

[2]

2 Use the information in the table to explain why Fiji is considered to be an MIC.

GDP per capita (2022)	$12 096
Inflation rate (2024)	4.8%
Tourist visitors (2023)	930 000
Population structure (2020)	Over 50% of population aged under 30; less than 10% aged over 60
Average household size (2020)	4.5
People living in poverty (less than $41.91/week) (2020)	24%
People living without piped water supply (2020)	34%
People using shared toilet facilities (2020)	5%

[4]

3 Imagine that you are a hotel owner in Fiji. Write six marketing points to encourage people to visit your hotel.

[6]

Skills link This sketch graph shows how the relationship between GDP per capita and life expectancy changes over time for Fiji. What has happened to the relationship between GDP per capita and life expectancy in Fiji over time?

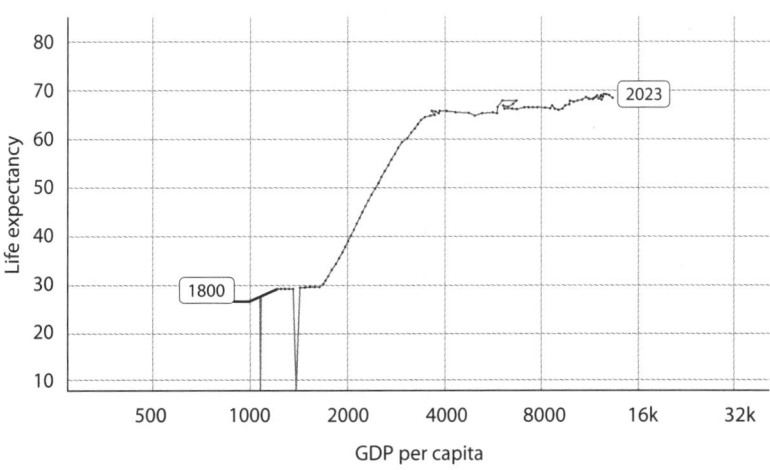

[3]

3.4 Changing economies

3.4.1 Classifying industry

Student's Book pages 278–87 | Syllabus learning objective 3.4

1 Complete the table with definitions and examples of different types of economic activity.

Sector	Definition	Example
Primary		
Secondary		
Tertiary		
Quaternary		

[8]

2 Look at the graph, which shows changes in sectors of employment in the UK between 1800 and 2000. Describe how employment has changed over time.

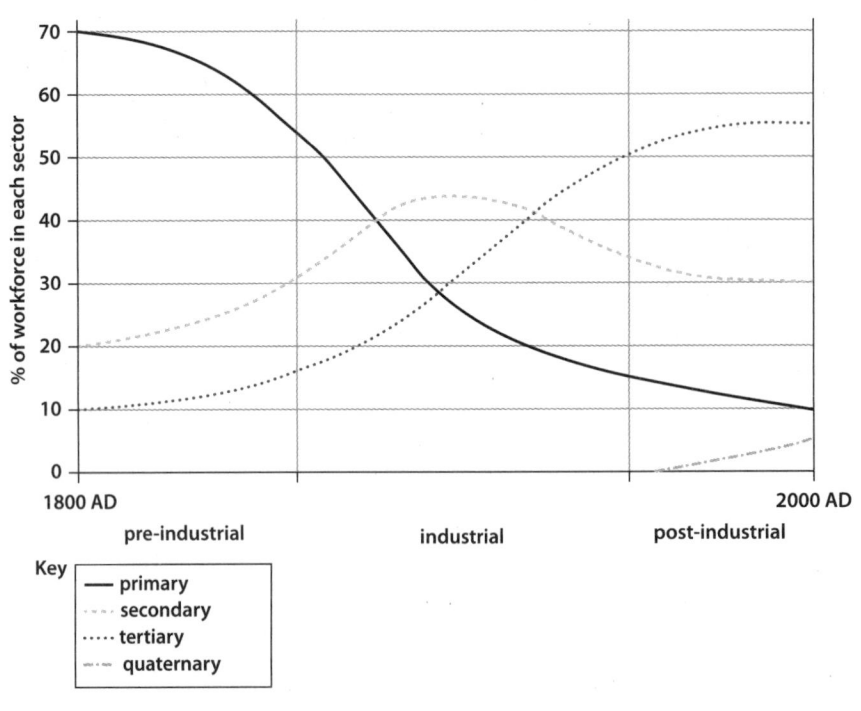

....

....

....

.... [4]

Skills link The container ship *Ever Given* blocked the Suez Canal for six days in March 2021 (below). Explain why this caused so many problems for global supply chains.

....

....

....

....

....

....

....

.... [6]

3.4.2 The impact of globalisation and the role of transnational corporations

Student's Book pages 288–95 | Syllabus learning objective 3.4

1 Define the term globalisation.

....

....

....

.... [2]

2 Globalisation brings a variety of positive and negative impacts. Imagine a conversation between two people; one of them believes that globalisation provides important benefits; the other thinks it has a negative impact.

Positive	Negative
Globalisation can	Yes, but ....
....	....
....	....
.... [4]	.... [4]

3 Xing works on the production line of a factory owned by a transnational corporation. Suggest two positive aspects of TNCs and two negative aspects of TNCs that might affect Xing.

....

....

....

....

....

.... [4]

Skills link Look at the table which shows merchandise exports for China in 2021. Answer the following questions.

Importing country/region	Merchandise exports from China (%)
Hong Kong	22
Japan	21
United States	18
Korea	5
Germany	4
Singapore	3
Netherlands	2
United Kingdom	2
Taiwan	2
France	1

- Which country does China export most goods to? .... [1]

- What percentage of its exports does China export to this country? .... [1]

- Which continent receives most of China's exports? .... [1]

- Why do you think this is the case? .... [1]

3.4.3 DSE Impacts of globalisation on Costa Rica

Student's Book pages 295–98 | Syllabus learning objective 3.4

1 These are the answers, but what are the questions?

- 5 million [1]

- San José [1]

- 2 million [1]

- Nicaragua and Panama [1]

- Central America [1]

2 State **three** reasons why Costa Rica is an attractive location for TNCs.

1.

2.

3. [3]

3 TNCs have played a significant role in developing ecotourism in Costa Rica, which is now one of the world leaders in this sector. Imagine that you are setting up a new ecotourism resort in the country. How will you convince the leader of a TNC to invest in your project?

_____

_____

_____

_____

_____

_____

_____

_____ [6]

Skills link The KOF Globalisation Index measures the level of globalisation for different countries. The world average is 61.63 points and is based on data from 190 countries.

- Costa Rica's score in 1970 was 42.69 points

- Costa Rica's score in 2021 was 71.00 points

- This score was made up of three elements:

    o   Globalisation – 67.00

    o   Social globalisation – 73.00

    o   Political globalisation – 74.00

State **two** conclusions about Costa Rica's globalisation that you can draw from this data.

1. _____

_____

_____

2. _____

_____

_____ [4]

3.4.4 The growth of the tourist industry

Student's Book pages 298–307 | Syllabus learning objective 3.4

1 Complete these reasons for the increase in global tourism.

- In many countries wealth has increased ....

  .... [1]

- Improvements in transportation ....

  .... [1]

- Ageing populations in HICs and MICs ....

  .... [1]

- The internet, advertising and television have ....

  .... [1]

2 Write the stage of the Butler model that each statement refers to.

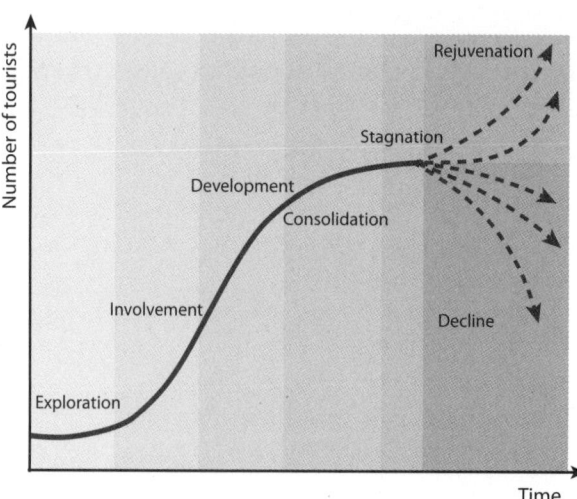

- .... Some locals express concern about rapid changes. [1]

- .... Hotels are converted to homes as tourist numbers plummet. [1]

- .... A few tourists discover a beach with no infrastructure. [1]

- .... The resort is no longer fashionable, relying on repeat visitors. [1]

- .... Tourism dominates the local economy. [1]

- .... There are more tourists and infrastructure is improved. [1]

- .... Major investment creates new attractions, for more visitors. [1]

3 Although sustainable tourism achieves real results in lowering environmental impacts and providing more benefits for local people, it still has problems. Explain each of the following issues in the context of sustainable tourism:

- Greenwashing ....

....

- Small-scale sustainable tourism ....

....

- Travel ....

....

- Limited benefits to local communities ....

[5]

Skills link Consider what fieldwork you would carry out to decide if a resort was sustainable. Think particularly about the data collection methods that you would use.

....

....

....

....

[4]

3.4.5 DSE Tourism in Iceland

Student's Book pages 308–12 | Syllabus learning objective 3.4

1 Use an atlas to locate the following tourist attractions in Iceland. Label these on the map.

- Reykjavík
- Blue Lagoon
- The Golden Circle
- Vatnajökull National Park
- Snæfellsnes Peninsula

[5]

2 State **two** benefits and **two** problems of tourism in Iceland.

[4]

Section 3: Human geography | 3.4 Changing economies

3 Imagine that you are a consultant to the Icelandic government. How would you suggest that they manage tourism in the country? Suggest **three** things that you would advise that they do and explain why they may help to reduce the issues that tourism creates.

[6]

Skills link Describe the pattern shown on the graph. Why do you think tourist numbers in Iceland dropped suddenly in 2020?

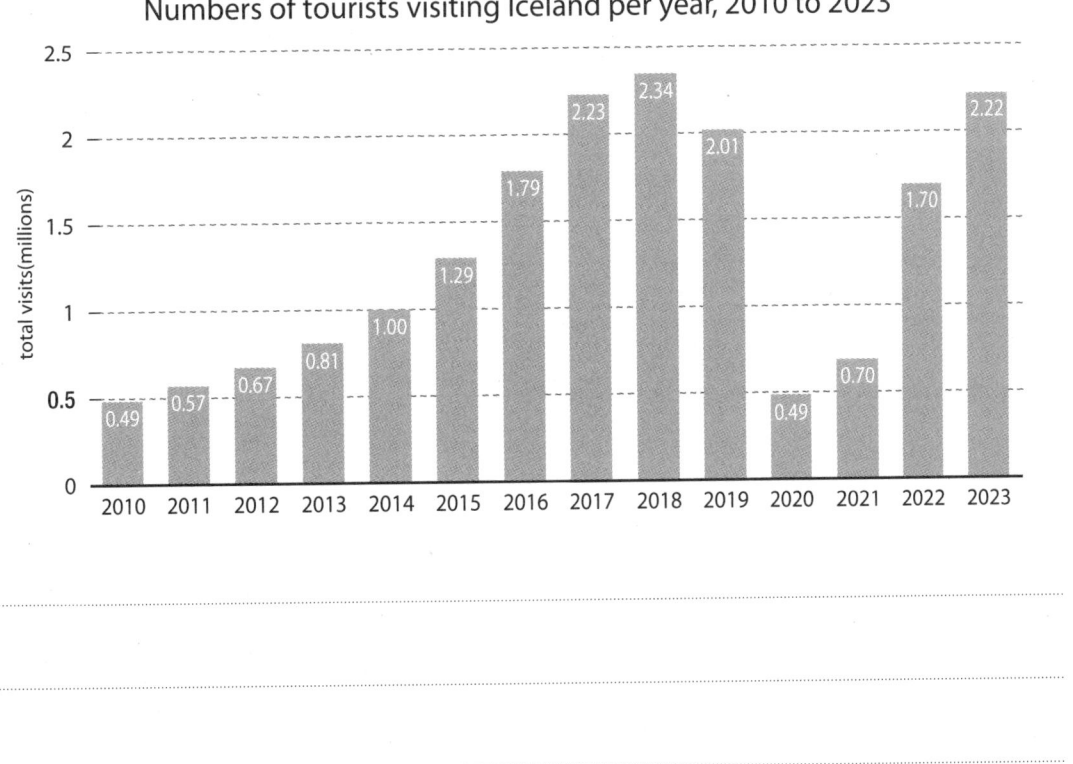

Numbers of tourists visiting Iceland per year, 2010 to 2023

[4]

3.5 Resource provision

3.5.1 How is our food produced?

Student's Book pages 318–24 | Syllabus learning objective 3.5

1 Look at the three different farmers in the table. Circle the correct description in each box to describe their type of farming.

Farmer	What we get out of the farm	What we put into the farm	What is grown
Farmer A farms goats and yams on a small plot of land. He grows just enough to feed his family and his farm doesn't have many inputs.	commercial / subsistence	intensive / extensive	arable / pastoral / mixed
Farmer B farms cows for dairy. He milks them twice a day using high-tech machinery and sells the milk for a profit.	commercial / subsistence	intensive / extensive	arable / pastoral / mixed
Farmer C farms wheat. She has invested a huge amount of money into pesticides and insecticides so that her produce is high-quality and buyers will purchase it for a profit.	commercial / subsistence	intensive / extensive	arable / pastoral / mixed

[9]

2 Explain **two** natural inputs to the farming system.

Natural inputs

1. ....

....

2. ....

....

[4]

3 Read the paragraphs below, which describe shifting cultivation. There are five mistakes. Can you spot and correct them? One whole sentence will need to be re-written.

In the Amazon and Congo rainforests some Indigenous communities carry out shifting cultivation. They build a small central village and farm crops in gardens nearby. When the soil quality starts to increase, they move their garden to a neighbouring area. Food crops grow easily so many inputs are needed, including the natural environment and large areas of land.

The most widespread form of subsistence farming is intensive wheat cultivation. It is a very high-yield crop and grows so fast that up to 10 crops can be harvested each year. As a result, there is a huge surplus.

Skills link Annotate the picture of a vertical hydroponic farm to highlight some of the inputs, processes and outputs of this farming system.

[4]

3.5.2 Investigating global patterns of food supply and demand

Student's Book pages 324–9 | Syllabus learning objective 3.5

1 Examine the map below and state **two** countries where the percentage of the population undernourished is above average and **two** countries where it is below average.

Above average:

1. ....

2. ....

Below average:

1. ....

2. .... [4]

2 Suggest **three** reasons why people choose to eat insect protein as part of their diet.

1. ....

2. ....

3. .... [3]

Section 3: Human geography | 3.5 Resource provision

3 How might a country's diet change as its population becomes more affluent? Draw food on the two plates and annotate them to explain these changes.

Less affluent country's diet

More affluent country's diet

[3]

3.5.3 The challenges of food supply

Student's Book pages 329–35 | Syllabus learning objective 10.3

1 Governments have an important role in causing and dealing with food shortages. Match the two halves of the sentences below to show how government investment can deal with the factors affecting food supply.

Provide an efficient infrastructure for distribution…	…so that farmers can maximise the supply of food.
Invest money in farming, such as loans or equipment…	…that can lead to people being deprived of food.
Restore degraded soils and replant the habitats used by pollinators…	…so that food can be transported quickly to those areas that need it.
Avoid wars and conflicts…	…rather than concentrating on growing food for export.
Make sure that land is available to grow locally eaten food crops…	…to be handed out when drought or natural disaster happens.
Build up reserves of food when it is available…	…to prioritise sustainable farming practices.

[6]

2 Food aid is one way of overcoming short-term food insecurity, particularly following a hazard. However, some argue that it can have a negative impact on the food supply system. Write a conversation between two people; one who believes food aid is important and the other who thinks it has a negative impact.

Positive	Negative
	[4]

3 Using the example of the Great Green Wall, explain how strategies such as this can slow desertification.

....

....

....

.... [4]

....

Skills link Using an atlas, label the deserts marked on the map below. Also, label three countries that are suffering from desertification.

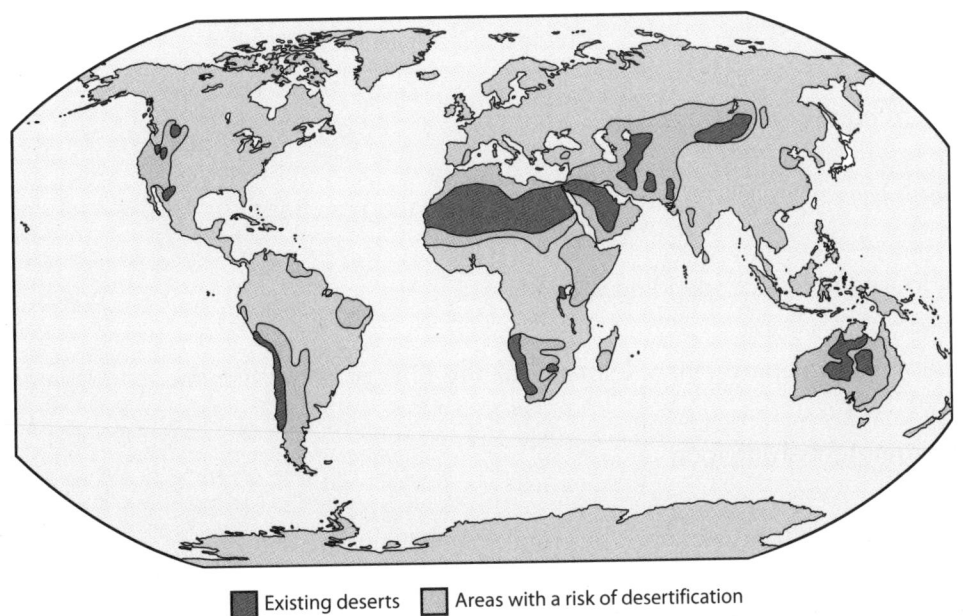

■ Existing deserts   ■ Areas with a risk of desertification

World Desertification

[6]

3.5.4 DSE Australia's changing food security

Student's Book pages 336–8 | Syllabus learning objective 3.5

1 Read the following statements and decide whether each is true or false.

1. Australia has over 2 million farms. ....

2. Australia imports 71% of its food. ....

3. Agriculture accounts for 75% of Australia's water usage. ....

4. Water security is made worse during El Niño years. ....

5. A government report in 2020 said that Australia was one of the least food secure nations in the world. ....

[5]

2 Complete the sentences.

1. By 2023, households across Australia began to show signs of food ....

2. Price .... affected people unequally.

3. There is a rising dependency on food ....

4. By October 2023, 3.7 million households were struggling to afford .... food.

5. Families looked to reduce spending with rising .... prices.

6. The government's Department of Climate Change, Energy, the Environment and Water has set targets for halving food ....

7. The logistics of food transport need to be improved, including the ...., which ensures refrigerated food doesn't defrost in transit.

[7]

3 Explain why it is important to take notice of Aboriginal and Torres Strait Islanders' views and knowledge of food security.

[4]

Skills link Look at the doughnut graphs, which show Australia's average food exports between 2015 and 2018. Then answer the following questions:

1. What agricultural product is exported the most? ....

2. Which agricultural product is exported the least? ....

3. What percentage of wheat is exported? ....

4. What percentage of dairy products are exported? ....

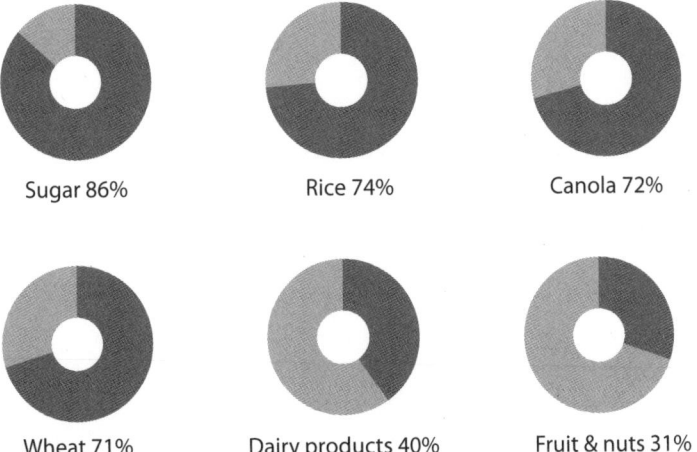

Sugar 86%   Rice 74%   Canola 72%

Wheat 71%   Dairy products 40%   Fruit & nuts 31%

[4]

3.5.5 How is our energy produced?

Student's Book pages 338–9 | Syllabus learning objective 3.5

1 ▶ Think about a typical day in your life. Write down as many things as you can that require electricity around the lightbulb.

[4]

2 ▶ Higher or lower? Look at the pie chart, which shows the worldwide generation of electricity by fuel source. For each type of energy, say whether the percentage of energy generated is higher or lower than the one before. The first one is done for you. Can you complete the chain?

1. Hydro – **14.28%**

2. Bioenergy – **Lower (2.30%)**

3. Gas

4. Coal

5. Oil

6. Solar

7. Nuclear

8. Wind

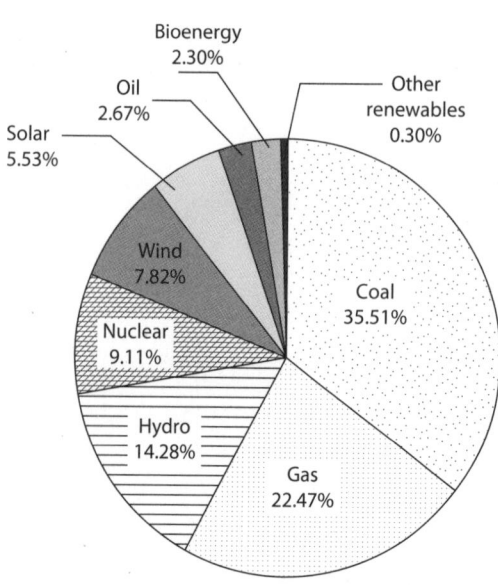

[6]

3 Why do you think that increasingly, sources of energy other than fossil fuels, are being used to generate electricity? Think about factors like climate and the time taken to produce energy sources in your answers.

....

....

....

.... [3]

Skills link Look at the data below, which show the energy mix of four countries in 2017: the US, Australia, Canada and the UK. They are all examples of HICs but have very different energy mixes. Answer the questions about them below.

US	Australia	Canada	UK
14% Coal	32% Coal	6% Coal	5% Coal
37% Oil	38% Oil	35% Oil	35% Oil
29% Gas	25% Gas	33% Gas	38% Gas
11% Renewables	6% Renewables	17% Renewables	10% Renewables
9% Nuclear	0% Nuclear	9% Nuclear	11% Nuclear

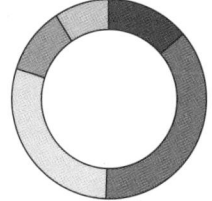 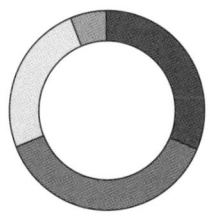 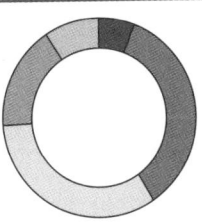 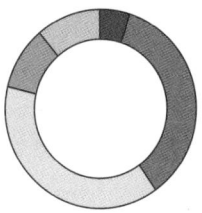

1. Which country uses the most renewables? ....

2. Which country uses the most nuclear energy? ....

3. Which country uses the least gas? ....

4. Which country uses the most fossil fuels? .... [4]

103

3.5.6 What are the global patterns of energy supply and demand?

Student's Book pages 339–46 | Syllabus learning objective 3.5

1 Why is Iceland able to produce most of its energy (90%) from geothermal power stations?

....

....

.... [2]

2 Draw a cartoon strip to illustrate the impacts of the fuelwood crisis.

Removing trees leaves soils open to erosion by wind and water. Farmers can't grow crops.	As wood becomes more scarce, people have to travel further to find it.
In urban areas, people may have to buy fuelwood, but as supplies get harder to find, prices rise.	Cooking with fuelwood in enclosed spaces causes breathing difficulties.

[4]

3 Name **two** countries that use a large amount of electricity and give a reason why they are a big consumer.

Country 1.

Country 2.

[4]

Skills link Answer the following questions using the map below which shows global movements and locations of fossil fuels.

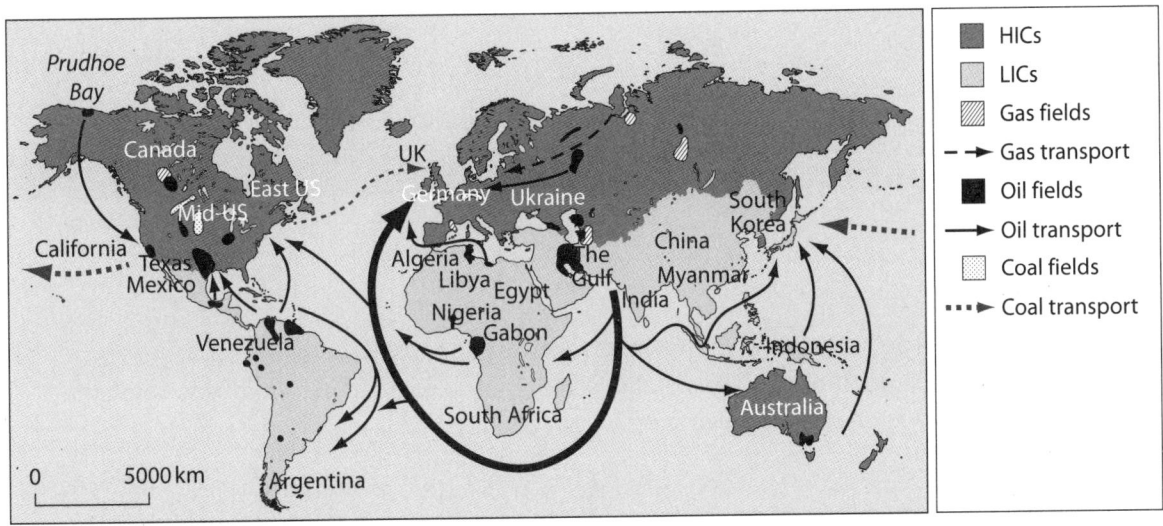

What is this type of map called?

[1]

Which region exports the most oil?

[1]

Why do you think this is?

[2]

Section 3: Human geography | 3.5 Resource provision

3.5.7 The impacts of energy production

Student's Book pages 347–50 | Syllabus learning objective 3.5

1 Look at the landscape in the photograph below. What are the advantages and disadvantages of generating energy in this way? Annotate the photograph with at least **two** advantages and **two** disadvantages.

[4]

2 Fossil fuels such as coal, oil and gas have advantages and disadvantages too. Write two advantages and two disadvantages on the scales below. To what extent do you think the advantages outweigh the disadvantages?

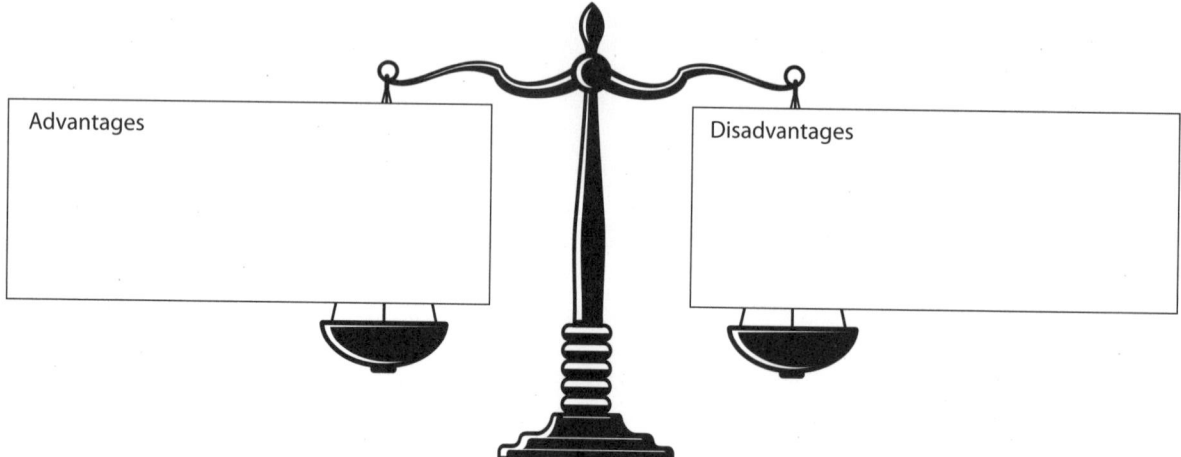

[4]

3 Why do you think that nuclear power is often seen as being controversial? Give **two** reasons.

....

....

....

.... [2]

Skills link Look closely at this chart which shows proportions of energy types used in the UK in 2022.

Domestic	Industry		Commercial		Energy industry	
	Other industries 11%		Shops 7%		Losses 9%	
	Engineering 5%	Food etc 3%			Used for generation 5%	Other energy industry 2%
			Offices 6%	Other commercial 5%	**Other**	
	Chemicals 4%	Paper etc 3%			Public admin 5%	Transport 3%
Domestic 29%		Iron & Steel 1%	Hotels 2%			Agriculture 1%

■ Domestic ■ Industry ■ Commercial ■ Other ■ Energy industry

Do you think this is a helpful way of presenting data showing the UK's energy usage?

.... [1]

Why do you think this?

....

....

....

....

.... [2]

Section 3: Human geography | 3.5 Resource provision

3.5.8 DSE Portugal's renewable energy

Student's Book pages 350–2 | Syllabus learning objective 3.5

1 Why does Portugal have good potential for wind and solar energy?

....

....

....

.... [2]

2 What questions can you ask about the Tâmega hydro electric power project? Write some geographical questions using the sentence starters to help you.

Who ....

What ....

Where ....

When ....

Why ....

How ....

What might ....

What should .... [8]

3 'If Portugal is able to generate 85% of its energy from renewables by 2030 then other countries should be able to achieve this too.'

To what extent do you agree with this statement? Mark your position on the continuum arrow and below write down three reasons for your answer.

[4]

Skills link Using the graph below, give two differences between Portugal's energy mix in 2000 and its energy mix in 2023.

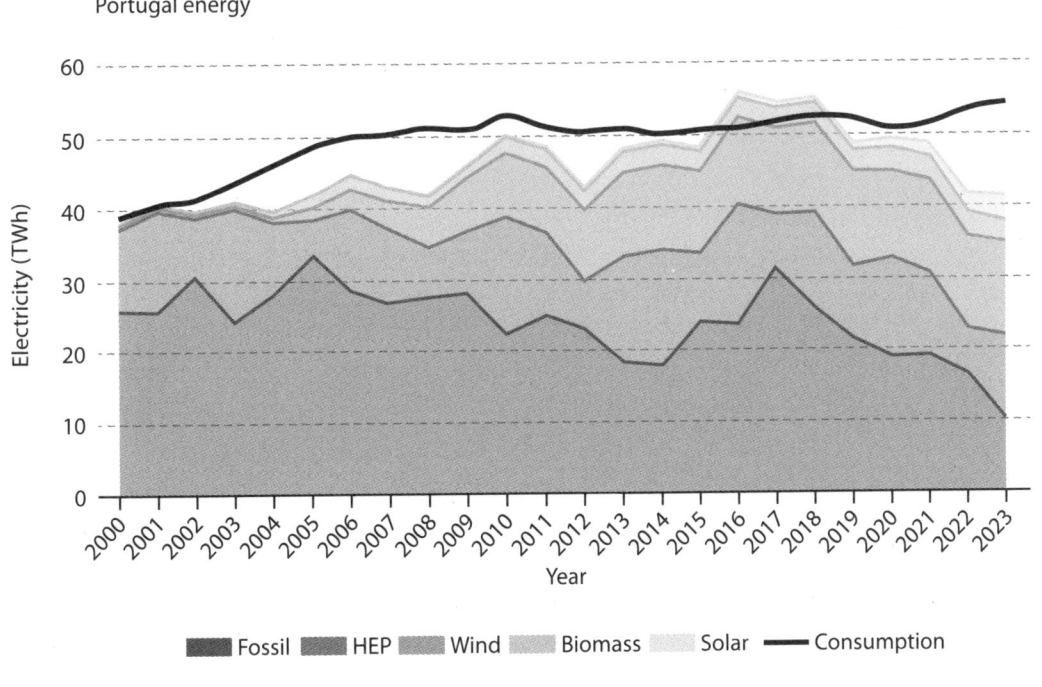

[2]

Acknowledgements

The publishers gratefully acknowledge the permission granted to reproduce the copyright material in this book. Every effort has been made to trace copyright holders and to obtain their permission for the use of copyright material. The publishers will gladly receive any information enabling them to rectify any error or omission at the first opportunity.

p.9 Doug McCutcheon / LGPL / Alamy Stock Photo; p.11 Toby Grayson / Shutterstock; p.12 Ranimiro Lotufo Neto / Shutterstock; p.21 Muhammad Adeel Ahmed / Shutterstock; p.22 Piperuk / Shutterstock; p.23 zelvan / Shutterstock; p.24 Pat Bonish / Alamy Stock Photo; p.25 Associated Press / Alamy Stock Photo; p.27 Source: NOAA; p.28 udaix / Shutterstock; p.33 Refox Photos / Shutterstock; p.35l&r NASA Earth Observatory; p.40 Wirestock Creators / Shutterstock; p.41 United States Geological Survey; p.44 samoila ionut / Shutterstock; p.45 Based on Web Map by navigatio2; p.49 Thorir Ingvarsson / Shutterstock; p.53 www.statista.com/chart/26117/average-number-of-internal-climate-migrants-by-2050-per-region; p.56 BublikHaus / Shutterstock; p.57 From: Bannan, D.; Ólafsdóttir, R.; Hennig, B.D. Local Perspectives on Climate Change, Its Impact and Adaptation: A Case Study from the Westfjords Region of Iceland. Climate 2022, 10, 169. https://doi.org/10.3390/cli10110169; p.65 Emmily / Shutterstock; p.65 GoodMan_Ekim / Shutterstock; p.71 Holger Mette / iStockphoto; p.72 Calin-H / Shutterstock; p.75 Source: UN World Population Review; p.76 Source: UK Office of National Statisics; p.77 Source: World Bank; p.79 Gapminder; p.83 Gapminder; p.84 Source: UK Office of National Statisics; p.85 Corona Borealis Studio / Shutterstock; p.88 Juhku / Shutterstock; p.94 asantosg / Shutterstock; p.94 © Road Genius; p.95 YEINISM / Shutterstock; p.97t schankz / Shutterstock; p.97b Kittima05 / Shutterstock; p.101 Draw Man / Shutterstock; p.101 Source: ABARES; p.102t kichikimi / Shutterstock; p.103 https://www.statista.com/chart/17437/energy-consumption-us-uk-australia-canada/; p.106t Snapshot freddy / Shutterstock; p.106b Buch and Bee / Shutterstock; p.107 Office of National Statistics; p.109 APREN © – The Portuguese Renewable Energy Association.